The Daily T

LOIRE VALLEY

in a week

MARTIN SYMINGTON

eadway · Hodder & Stoughton

Acknowledgements

The author and publishers are grateful to the following for permission to
reproduce photographs in this volume:

J Allan Cash Ltd: p 95; Food and Wine from France: pp 26, 41, 63, 112, 116;
West Loire Tourist Board: pp 5, 13, 22, 59; West Loire Tourist Board, Nicole
Lejeune: pp 24, 83, 114, Back cover

All other photographs taken by the author

Maps created by Alan Gilliland and Glenn Swann

Front cover: Château de la Ferté-St Aubin in the Sologne
Back cover: Sunflowers in the Loire Valley

British Library Cataloguing in Publication Data
Symington, Martin
"Daily Telegraph" Loire Valley in a Week
("Daily Telegraph" Travel in a Week Series)
I. Title II. Series
914.4504

ISBN 0 340 58317-7

First published 1993
Third impression 1993

© 1993 The Telegraph plc

Printed in Italy for the educational publishing division of Hodder & Stoughton
Ltd, Mill Road, Dunton Green, Sevenoaks, Kent by New Interlitho, Milan.

LOIRE VALLEY IN A WEEK

Introduction

This guide is designed for visitors touring the Loire Valley by car who want to select the best the region has to offer in the limited time at their disposal. The river valley and its delightful tributaries have been divided into seven areas, each of which can easily be covered in a day's drive. Within each of these 'Days' the most interesting sights, from the major châteaux and historic towns to the great vineyards of the Loire, have been arranged in alphabetical order for easy reference. From the Day's menu you can choose the attractions which hold most appeal, depending on the weather, your interests, and whether you are travelling with children. Symbols placed alongside the text will aid you in your choice.

There are over 100 châteaux in the Loire Valley, ranging from defensive fortresses and splendid Renaissance masterpieces to smaller stately homes filled with beautiful furniture. We have made a highly critical appraisal of all those open to the public, selecting only those which genuinely reward a visit. We have also sought out places to enjoy some of the region's simpler pleasures - riverbank walks, swimming opportunities and scenic places for a picnic - which have been highlighted in the text.

The quest of the wine lover has been taken seriously, with suggestions for visiting vineyards, tasting and buying the outstanding and diverse wines of the Loire. At the end of each Day we have given suggestions for places to stay, ranging from château-hotels to inexpensive *auberges*, and places to enjoy either *haute cuisine* or simpler regional fare, depending on your budget.

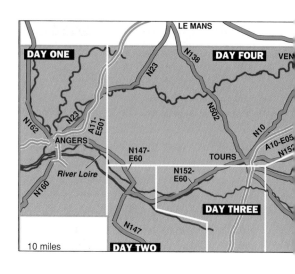

KEY TO SYMBOLS

⊛ Star Attraction

☆ Well worth a visit

☆ Of interest

❗ Walk of the day

🚗 Drive of the day

═══ Route of drive

☀ Fine weather attraction

🌧 Wet weather attraction

🏃 Enjoyable for children

ⓘ Tourist Office

◉ Lunch/snack stop

🍷 Wine-tasting

🏠 Hotel

CH Chambres d'Hôte

✗ Restaurant

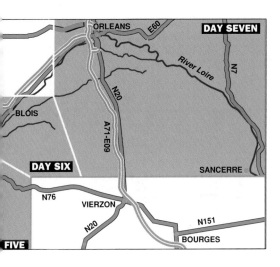

 Credit cards accepted

 Credit cards not accepted

£   Bed and breakfast under £15 per person; three-course meal under £10 a head

££   Bed and breakfast £16-£30 per person; three-course meal £11-£16 a head

£££   Bed and breakfast £31-£49 per person; three-course meal £17-£24 a head

££££ Bed and breakfast over £50 per person; three-course meal over £25 a head

CONTENTS

LOWER
ANJOU

The river Loire slices through the ancient Dukedom of Anjou, whose history is so intertwined with that of England. King Henry II spent most of his reign in Angers from where he consolidated the Plantagenet family's Anglo-Angevin Empire, which eventually crumbled in the Hundred Years War.

Angers was the fortress capital of Anjou and today still holds a concentration of the region's historical sites. A very full day could be spent in the city's old quarter alone, exploring the castle, cathedral and mediaeval streets which together amount to a cornerstone of the Loire's history.

Three main tributaries join the Loire near Angers. They flow through some sleepy, pretty backwaters, well away from the tourist trail: anglers, casual walkers and nature-lovers relax in north Anjou. Even if the weather lets you down, the area makes picturesque touring and you can take in the less-visited châteaux of Montgeoffroy and Plessis-Bourré. A peaceful day can be crowned by a visit to Solesmes Abbey to be transported by the other-worldly tones of Gregorian plainchant.

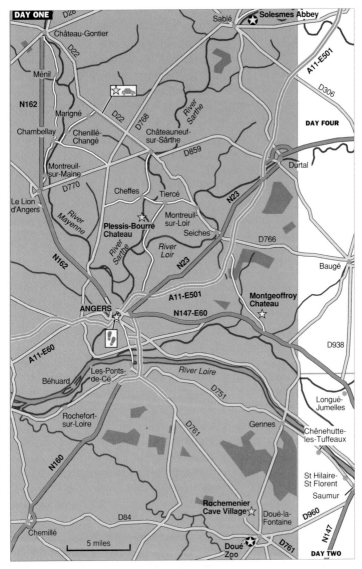

Anjou south of the Loire is very different again. The flat, open,
farmland lacks the leafy calm of the Sarthe and Maine valleys,
but is coloured by local characteristics such as its great stone
windmills and acres of rose nurseries. Anyone with children has
an excellent excuse to visit the unusual zoo at Doué.

☆ ANGERS

Angers stands in stark contrast to the graceful architecture of the Loire Valley's Renaissance era. Here is a mediaeval city, dominated by the grim, warlike battlements of its defensive castle, perched on a cliff above the Maine, a tributary of the Loire. An assault on Angers must have been a daunting prospect for the warriors of the Middle Ages.

Today, penetrating Angers' old town involves an unpromising journey through the high-rise suburban sprawl which encircles the city, with the possibility of getting snarled up in the traffic which chokes the tangle of outskirt roads.

 Don't be put off; once you reach the city's historic kernel, compressed into a small area round the château, all the sights are within a short walk. Follow signs to *Le Château*, outside which, on Place Kennedy, is a large car park and an uncommonly helpful **Tourist Office** (tel: 41 88 69 93).

Five hundred years ago the dry moat surrounding the **Château d'Angers** (you'd never get water up there, high above the river) was filled with King René's collection of leopards, lions and other hungry wild animals. Nowadays, immaculately tended formal gardens surround the forbidding walls with just a few fallow deer amid the topiary. The entrance to the château is a single drawbridge spanning the moat, with the ticket office beneath a heavy black portcullis.

Unexpectedly, inside are more formal gardens, mini avenues of yew trees and a white tufa-stone chapel, all in peaceful contrast with the castle's dark, austere exterior and the 17 gigantic bastions enclosing the fortress. You can climb up any one of these towers on to the ramparts and walk round the perimeter – a total of over a kilometre – for some spectacular views over the city, the River Maine and the great sweep of the Loire flood-plain beyond.

There is no better example of a warlike, feudal château than this in all the Loire. Most of the structure which stands today was built in the early 13th century by Louis IX, on the foundations of a fortress held by the redoubtable Foulques Nerra 300 years previously. The gardens were built by 'Good King René', the 15th-century Count of Anjou whose mother, Yolande of Aragon, added the chapel.

Château d'Angers

It would take years to gain an expert appreciation of the artistic skills behind the major works of tapestry in the châteaux of the Loire. But for an eye-opening glimpse of how great an art-form tapestry can be, you have only to stand before the **Apocalypse Tapestry**. It was sewn in Paris for Louis I, Duke of Anjou, over ten continuous years beginning in 1373. Its purpose was to inspire faith in persecuted Christians with dramatic illustrations of the last book of the bible, St. John's Revelation, complete with scenes of ghastly torment in hell as well as unfathomable bliss awaiting the blessed.

The tapestry originally extended 130 metres – that's longer than a full-sized football pitch - divided into six sections, each depicting seven biblical scenes. During the French Revolution, when Angers was sacked, it was thrown on to the street and parts of it burned. However, most of the pieces were subsequently retrieved and more than two thirds of the original is on view in a tasteful, modern building within the castle walls.

The biblical passages next to the relevant pieces of tapestry are in French only, as are most of the guided tours. However, half-hour-long English audio-tapes are available to guide you through the tapestry, or you may be lucky enough to join the occasional English tour conducted when there is a sufficiently large group.

Even if the very idea of an old tapestry makes you yawn, don't miss this one.

There is a small café serving light refreshments within the castle walls.

Château d'Angers. Tel: 41 87 43 47
Opening times: daily all year 9am-7pm
Admission: adult 31F; child 16F

'The Cathedral is happy to welcome the anglophone visits at the core of the city'. With so assuring an invitation posted on the front door of the fine 12th- and 13th-century Gothic **Cathedral of St Maurice**, who could pass it by?

First have a look at the spectacular carved stone façade, from the top of a long flight of steps down to the River Maine. By contrast, the interior is dark and gloomy, causing some people to spend no more than five minutes inside, although in summer others shelter in its delicious coolness. Once your eyes have become accustomed to the meagre light, however, there are some wonders to explore. In particular, the Gothic vaulting is one of the earliest examples in Europe of this much-copied style; some of the stained glass windows are 12th-century originals, disfigured with age; and the treasury (on the left as you enter the main door) has a collection of gold and siver chalices among other interesting exhibits, such as a green marble Roman bath.

As for the 'welcomed anglophone visits', there are a few wall-mounted explanations, written in surprisingly good English.

Entrance is free, but donations for up-keep are appealed for. There are no published opening or closing times, although the cathedral is locked at night

A WALK AROUND THE OLD TOWN OF ANGERS

The Tourist Information Office, opposite the Place Kennedy car park in the shadow of the castle, will supply a map of the old town and plenty of suggestions for things to see and do.

The mediaeval old town is a tight little area where you are never far from the castle or cathedral. It is made up of paved and cobbled streets, pedestrian precincts, quaint old buildings, some of them housing chic modern shops, and countless terrace cafés. The city is at its liveliest during academic term-time when there is a crowded, colourful but unhurried atmosphere as the University presence asserts itself. Café tables become weighed down with books while their owners chatter and sip coffee;

others sit playing their guitars on the long flight of steps leading from the river up to the cathedral.

As you meander through the arcane back streets connecting various tiny squares, there are several points of interest not to miss. Look out for the **Chapelle Toussaint**, a 13th-century chapel with a new glass roof, which houses a collection of original casts by David d'Angers, the city's famous 19th-century sculptor. In Place St Croix, just behind the cathedral, is the **Maison d'Adam**, a large 15th-century house decorated with some intricate carved figures, and looking decidedly wobbly on its ancient timber frame.

Les Halles, almost next to the Cathedral, is a covered food market where many of the stalls serve simple lunchtime meals. You can snack on cheese, cold meats or seafood in a noisy, colourful atmosphere, surrounded by the competing smells of fish, fruit and coffee. On narrow Rue Musée is the **Musée des Beaux Arts** in a fine Renaissance mansion, the Logis Barrault. The house is worth seeing for itself, although the small collection of art, including a Raphael, merits some time. End up on the lively Place du Ralliement, the centre of town, watching the world go by from a café terrace.

Angers: Skyline   *Old town*

The **Vinotèque** in Angers, directly opposite the château entrance, promotes Anjou and Touraine wines with piles of literature and has a bar where you can taste free samples of what are considered to be the best examples of each type. Somehow, even the usually bland Rosé d'Anjou tastes fruitily subtle.

DOUE ZOO

The former tufa stone quarry which houses this zoo is a remarkable phenomenon in itself. Over ten acres of quarries, pits, tunnels, troglodyte caves, streams, lakes and islands have been put to imaginative use to create a habitat for the animals in a cross between a conventional zoo and a walk-in safari park.

Although the big cats and other dangerous species are kept at a safe distance in large, landscaped enclosures, their behaviour can be observed from camouflaged hides. Camels, giraffes and zebras in open expanses are separated from the public by just a fence, rather like cattle or horses on a farm. The monkeys live on islands, with just water and the visitors' trails between them and nets strung across quarries form cavernous, walk-in aviaries. Lush vegetation and beautiful flowers line the trails which cross bridges and go underground through seeping tunnels; in places you can feel as if you are in a rainforest. The overall effect is to allow the animals to be discreetly observed, rather than gawped at by visitors.

Curiously, soft classical music is piped into the background. This can be a bit off-putting if you are trying to listen to the soft purring of a tiger cub, but perhaps the animals like it.

There is also a mini-zoo on site with farm animals, including dwarf goats and pigs, for very small children, who with adult supervision can go in to the pens and touch them, and a rainforest exhibition designed to heighten consciousness of environmental and conservation issues.

A small snack-bar within the zoo is open all day for light refreshments.

Jardin Zoologique, off the D690 west of Doué-la-Fontaine. Tel: 41 59 18 58
Opening times: daily 9am–7pm in summer, 9am–noon & 2–6 pm in winter
Admission: adult 45F, child 20F

Doué Zoo

The flat, open countryside around Doué-la-Fontaine is one of the most important places in France for cultivating roses. From May through to July you can drive through vast expanses of vivid fragrant blooms. Just outside Doué, on the D84 is a **Jardin des Roses**, open to the public; in mid-July a rose festival is held in Doué.

 ## MONTGEOFFROY CHATEAU

The charm of this relatively minor château is that it is still the home of the family for whom it was built in the late 18th century.

A huge wrought-iron gate stands at the entrance, from where a long, straight, gravelled drive leads dramatically up to the stately mansion, boldly designed with a classical elegance which turned its back almost entirely on the turrets and crenellations which were still prevalent in the architecture of its era.

There are acres of parkland to wander around and, in the stables, a small exhibition of gleaming carriages, saddles and other horsey paraphernalia. On the château tour itself, you are ushered through commodious, panelled rooms of exquisite furniture, all of which is the original. Every now and then, amid the historic paintings and tapestries, you might find touching tell-tale signs, such as bottom-imprints in cushions, of the château's other role as a family home between the daily influx of visitors.

Be warned, however. You can go round only by waiting for the next tour group, and spending at least 45 minutes inside while a full history of the château, its contents, and the de Contades family is recounted in French by a fastidiously conscientious guide. A ring-bound file with English translations is available and can be carried round, but it wouldn't be cricket to decide half-way through that you wanted out. Not in a private home.

Château de Montgeoffroy, on the D74 north of Mazé. Tel: 41 80 60 02
Opening times: daily Mar–Nov, 9.30am–6.30pm
Admission: adult 35F; child 25F

LE PLESSIS-BOURRE CHATEAU

Out in the flat, watery meadowland between the rivers Sarthe and Mayenne stands this fortified, 15th-century home looking like a stern, yet graceful white ship at anchor in the middle of a lake.

For anyone following the evolution of the Loire château from warlike, defensive fortress to elegant Renaissance residence, here is one of the best links between the two to be found anywhere. Its towers still had a genuine defensive purpose and the wide moat, crossed by a multi-spanned bridge nearly 50 yards long, was built as protection to compensate for not being on high ground. But the stern lines of a fortress have been softened, the towers are rounded, and the moat is really a small lake.

The spacious courtyard is beautifully proportioned, but there are austere stone staircases up to the towers and a gloomy dungeon prison providing further evidence of the feudal practices which persisted into the early Renaissance age. It was built for Jean Bourré, childhood tutor to King Louis XI.

Fittingly for a fairly minor château well away from any other architectural site, the tour is relaxed and unstuffy. Friendly and personable guides such as you find here make all the difference to a château visit. Being out-of-the-way, it's also refreshingly uncrowded, even on weekdays. With masses of precious furniture, paintings and panelling around, however, you are not allowed to wander alone.

Don't miss the bizarre panelling on the ceiling of the *Salle des Gardes*, on which are depicted all kinds of strange allegorical and moralistic stories. Some of the favourite but least comprehensible of these include a full-breasted, naked woman at the helm of a wheeled land yacht, and the row of contented-looking people standing in a line relieving themselves.

Château du Plessis-Bourré, signposted from Cheffes on the D74. Tel: 41 32 06 01
Opening times: daily 10am–noon and 2–7pm during Jul and Aug; 10am-noon and
2–5pm the rest of the year; closed Wednes and Thurs mornings
Admission: adult 30F, child 7-18 20F

> At Montreuil-sur-Loir you can drive down a steep, dead-end hill by taking the only left-hand turning off the D 74 in the village as you drive towards Seiches. At the bottom is a sublime **picnic spot** in a meadow bordered by the poplar-lined River Loir, and beside a shady wood carpeted with wild flowers.

ROCHEMENIER CAVE VILLAGE

In subterranean contrast to the great châteaux which have been turned into museums, here you can see the way of life of another of the Loire Valley's dwelling traditions – underground homes in caves and quarries. The majority of these so-called 'troglodyte' homes are cut into cliff-sides. However, at Rochemenier, south-west of Doué-la-Fontaine, a village grew up in a white, tufa-stone quarry beneath the surface of a wide, flat plain.

Until the 1930s the underground village was inhabited by farm-ing families who lived, worked, prayed and made merry down in the quarry with bedrooms, kitchens, communal areas, wine cellars, quarters for their animals and a large chapel in the shape of a cross, all dug out of the soft rock.

You can wander freely around the 20 rooms which make up the exhibition. Furniture, artefacts, and ornaments are still in place in each one, with explanations painting a romantic picture of life underground, including photographs of these proud folk at work and play.

However much cave-dwelling may evoke pre-historic images, a visit to this village makes a convincing case for life underground. These homes were cheap to construct and could have new wings and extensions added by simply hacking out some more rock. They were also secure, easy to heat during winter and naturally cool in summer. It makes you wonder why they ever moved out in favour of the more conventional, modern village which now stands next to its underground counterpart.

Village Troglodytique, Rochemenier-Louresse, north of Doué-la-Fontaine.
Tel: 41 59 18 15
Opening times: Jul and Aug, daily 9.30am–7pm; Apr–Jun, Sept and Oct, closed noon–2.30pm, (in Oct also closed all day Mon); Nov–Mar, open Sat and Sun only
Admission: adult 16F; child 10F

Troglodyte Museum at Rochemenier

At Rochemenier, next to the Troglodyte Museum, is a **café** serving copious helpings of homely, farmhouse-style *plats du jour*, such as pork casserole or rabbit stew, with local *vin du pays* served in jugs.

☆ SARTHE AND MAYENNE DRIVE

When you've had enough of sight-seeing and long to get out into the tranquillity of rural France, try meandering along the narrow lanes which follow the banks of the Sarthe and Mayenne. These are two tributaries which flow more or less due south to merge just north of Angers, before their confluence with the mighty Loire.

In part the region's charm lies in the fact that there are few major sights to visit in north Anjou. Anglers and nature lovers escape from the cities of the Loire to mess about in boats or just generally take life at a lazy pace in this easy-going back-water. There are countless enchanting routes one could take. Here is one of them.

Start at Lion d'Angers, on the N162 north of Angers. From here, take the narrow D187 northwards along the shaded banks of the gentle, green Mayenne through the tiny village of Montreuil to Chambellay, where you cross a stone bridge and turn left for Chenillé-Changé with its needle-spired church poking up through the surrounding greenery. Past the hamlet of Marigné, turn right on to the long, straight D859 through open acres of corn fields, to join the Sarthe at Châteauneuf-sur-Sarthe. Instead of crossing over, take the nameless lane which hugs the river bank on its way down to Cheffes – one of the most delightful villages in the region with rowing boats and bicycles (including children's bikes) for hire from a grassy bank by the water's edge. Fifty yards away is Place de l'Eglise – the main square – where there's a delicious *pâtisserie* and a *tabac* well-stocked with fishing tackle.

Fishing on the peaceful River Sarthe

From Cheffes, Château du Plessis-Bourré (see separate entry) is a short and worthwhile detour. Alternatively, cross the river and head for Tiercé, where a right turn takes you on to the D52 which crosses another tributary, Le Loir, and strikes across some marshland before getting lost in the outskirts of Angers.

⭐ SOLESMES ABBEY

If you're staying on the Loire, Solesmes Abbey, a little way upstream from Sablé-sur-Sarthe and a 45-minute drive from Angers, is rather out of the way. When you get there, the high, sturdy, prison-like abbey rises almost offensively from the gentle Sarthe riverscape. Why make the journey? For the chance to listen to the most beautiful Gregorian plainchant in the world.

The Benedictine monastery was founded in the 11th century, although the present abbey church and most of the buildings date only from the last century. Within the monastery walls you cross a courtyard to the church – the only part open to the public. Inside the simple church is a powerful scent of freshly-burned incense, a rare peacefulness and an atmosphere of quiet spirituality. Whether there are a few supplicant faithful about, or the church is totally empty, it is worth just sitting quietly for a moment. As the church is entirely sound-proof, the silence is total.

Solesmes Abbey

Every day at 9.45am and 1pm, 4.50pm, 7.00pm and 8.30pm, the cowled monks file into their stalls and begin their up-lifting, almost haunting Latin chant of the Divine Offices to gentle organ music. Even the thickest-skinned cannot fail to be moved by this. (On Sundays there is also sung Latin mass at 10am.) Records, tapes and compact discs of the world-famous plainchant are for sale in a shop on the way out.

A word of caution: you may be accosted by hangers-on with hard-luck stories outside the monastery gates. How you treat them is your business, but suffice it to say that there are probably more genuine and deserving causes around.

The Abbey church of Solesmes is open to the public during each of the Divine Offices and at all times in between. The three middle services last just 10-15 minutes each, the others about 30 minutes
Admission: free

WHERE TO STAY

Château-Gontier
⌂ ✕ ▬ £

Hostellerie de Mirwault, *Rue de Val de Mayenne, Bazouges, F-53200 Château-Gontier Tel: 43 07 13 17 H open all year; R closed Wednes* An English couple, William and Evelyn Mitchell, took over this Mayenne-side hotel in 1990 and have given the modern building a wonderfully relaxed atmosphere, with little touches such as fruit-baskets in the bedrooms, and restaurant tables arranged for best views over the river. The food is fresh, unfancy and delicious. Set in the village of Bazouches, outside the attractive old town of Château-Gontier, it is a sleepy, out-of-the-way little place and a good base for exploring the northern tributaries, off the classic château-beat of the Loire. Last orders: lunch 2.30pm; dinner 10pm.

Châteauneuf-sur-Sarthe
⌂ ✕ ▬ £

Hôtel de la Sarthe, *9, rue du Port, F-49330 Châteauneuf-sur-Sarthe Tel: 41 69 85 29 R closed Sun eve and Mon except Jul and Aug* A simple, ivy-covered Logis de France in a peaceful and charming spot overlooking a stretch of the Sarthe popular with anglers. The rooms are rustic, cheerful and welcoming. The dining-room is fairly basic but full of character; alternatively, you can eat out on the waterside terrace when it's fine. Much of the menu, including slimy but delicious Sarthe eels, comes from the river. Last orders: lunch, 2pm; dinner 9pm.

Montreuil-sur-Loir

⌂ ▭ *£*

Château de Montreuil, *Montreuil-sur-Loir, F-49140 Seiches-sur-le-Loir*
Tel: 41 76 21 03
Open mid-Mar to mid-Oct

Beyond the fine façade of this stately home turned into a *Chambres d'Hôte*, and looking grandly down on the Loir tributary, is the sort of welcome you get in the best English bed and breakfasts – very personal, but not intrusive. The owners, Monsieur and Madame Bailliou, are local farmers, not full-time hoteliers, and do not run a restaurant. Madame will, however, produce dinner on request. The rooms are comfortable if not luxurious, with an atmosphere more in keeping with an old farmhouse than a neo-Gothic château. All the rooms have shower cubicles, but loos are shared – one for every two rooms.

Les Ponts de Cé

⌂ ✕ ▭ *££*

Le Bosquet, *F-49130 les Ponts-de-Cé*
Tel: 41 57 72 42
Closed Sun eve and Mon

Just south of Angers, the Loire splinters into several strands, creating a series of long, serpentine islands before the waters reconverge. The modern Le Bosquet is on the southernmost of these islands with its back to the busy N160 which crosses the river and leads into Angers. The bed-

rooms at the front have an attractive view over the river and are comfortable, if otherwise unexceptional. The restaurant is exceptional, as evidenced by its huge popularity with locals. Have an *apéritif* on the riverside terrace, before going inside for a rich choice of regional specialities with the emphasis on fish, and mushrooms prepared in every way imaginable. Last orders: lunch, 2pm; dinner 10pm.

Solesmes

⌂ ✕ ▭ *££*

Grand Hôtel de Solesmes,
F-72300 Sablé/Solesmes
Tel: 43 95 45 10
H closed Feb; R closed Sun eve

If it wasn't for the sound-proofing in the abbey church, you would be able to hear the Gregorian plainchant wafting over the abbey walls and into this spanking clean modern hotel just across the road. The rooms are luxurious, each one carefully and differently decorated and furnished. There is a small, beautifully tended garden at the back, onto which some rooms have over-hanging balconies. The dining room is smart, serving exquisitely presented *nouvelle cuisine*-ish food. The River Sarthe and tow-path walks are only a short distance away. Last orders: lunch 2pm; dinner 9.30pm.

WHERE TO EAT

Angers
✕ 🚆 ££

Grand Cercle, *18, boulevard Maréchal-Foch, Angers*
Tel: 41 87 37 20
Open all year
Quality restaurants are hard to find in the heart of Angers' old town, although there are numerous lively cafés frequented by students. A walk away on the wide Boulevard Maréchal-Foch this large, unstuffy restaurant welcomes children. It is modern and extremely busy, mainly with locals; but the waiters have time to be personable and even suggest simple meals for the kids. There are plenty of salads and light dishes, making it ideal for lunch. The glistening seafood platter is mouthwatering. Last orders: lunch 2.30pm; dinner 10.30pm.

Angers
✕ 🚆 ££

La Terrace, *la Pointe Bouchemaine, Angers*
Tel: 41 77 11 96
Closed Sun eve and, Oct-May only, Mon
Book in advance and you stand a chance of getting one of the ten tables with expansive views over the Loire and the Maine. Just south of Angers, this is a recently-opened restaurant with simple, tasteful decor in tiny Bouchemaine, right on the confluence of the two rivers. The menu reflects the fishing traditions of the village; choose from turbot, eels, perch and seafood terrine as you watch anglers cast from their rowing boats in the

mouth of the river. Last orders: lunch, 1.30pm; dinner 9.30pm.

Béhuard
✕ 🚆 £

Le Grand Pont, *Béhuard, Angers*
Tel: 41 72 21 64
Closed Tues eve Sept-Mar
Béhuard is a delightful, small village on one of the large islands in the Loire, south of Angers. Le Grand Pont oozes rural character inside but has a pleasant terrace for fine weather. The set menu invariably includes local river fish; there is also a huge assortment of cheeses, including a few pongy goats' cheeses. Last orders: lunch 2.00pm, dinner 9pm.

Chenillé-Changé
✕ 🚆 ££

La Table du Meunier, *Chenillé-Changé, le Lion d'Angers*
Tel: 41 95 10 83
Closed Mon eve, Tues eve and Wednes, except Jul-Sept
If you are exploring the tow-paths of the Mayenne or the Sarthe on foot, or following the gentle lanes through the pastures between the two tributaries, La Table du Meunier makes a delightful lunch break. The small restaurant is housed in an old stone walnut press set back from the Mayenne. With five small dining rooms it has a homely feel to it; in summer you can sit out on the terrace. Specialities of the house include duck and goose dishes. Last orders: lunch, 2.00pm; dinner 10.00pm.

'WHITE' ANJOU
AND THE VIENNE

On the eastern flank of what is sometimes known as 'White Anjou', on account of the ubiquitous chalky tufa stone, is Saumur, dominated by its dazzling fortress Château. History seems to have conspired to prevent the town from blossoming into the large city which its early eminence suggested might have been inevitable. Instead, it has settled for being a manageably small place with a strangely divergent list of claims to fame: the mushroom capital of France; a nationally important equestrian centre; the home of a famous sparkling wine, and, of course, the fabulous Château. The joy of visiting Saumur – and nearby St Hilaire-St Florent – is the variety of things to see and do, whatever the weather.

Upstream in the extreme west of Touraine is another spectacular, fortress-topped city whose place in history outpaces its modern role as a wine town. This is Chinon, on the River Vienne, where the animated wine and cooperage museum is yet another example of an entertaining family attraction cleverly encapsulated within a local phenomenon. It would make the beautiful old city worth visiting even in the pouring rain. Just outside Chinon is a delightful stretch of the Vienne, cutting through expanses of vineyards in its course towards the Loire some 15 kilometres downsteam.

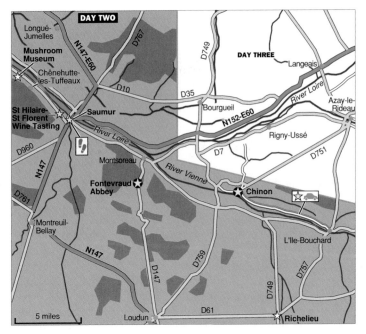

On the white-speckled plains, roughly half-way between Saumur and Chinon, is Fontevraud Abbey, one of the most fascinating historical sites in the Loire, especially for the English who can visit the tombs of two of their kings.

✪ CHINON

The grim and forbidding ruined castle which dominates small, compact Chinon gives it a harsh mien when viewed from a distance. This softens into quaintness as you explore the perfectly restored mediaeval lower town, wedged between the river and the soaring cliffs crowned by the crenellated castle. With luck you should be able to park along the quayside, within a short walk of the Place de l'Hôtel de Ville – the hub for visiting both castle and old town.

Chinon was one of the principal strongholds of Henry Plantaganet (Henry II of England) who died here in 1189, before being taken to Fontevraud for burial. Chinon's importance was

Chinon and the River Vienne

eclipsed when King John lost his French possessions, but the town still punctuates the history of France. It was in Chinon that Joan of Arc recognised the disguised Dauphin in 1429; François Rabelais, the rebellious and irreverent author, was born here in 1494; and the all-powerful Cardinal Richelieu, Louis XIII's Prime Minister over a century later, owned the castle. It was he who was largely responsible for its ruin, by taking its stones to build the new town which was to bear his name, 24 kilometres away. There are no tapestries, paintings or *objets d'art* in the **Château de Chinon**. This is the raw shell of a real, ruined fortress which belonged to the Counts of Blois before being captured by their enemies, the Counts of Anjou, when its mediaeval heyday began.

It's a stiff climb from the main square, up some beautiful old stone steps. It is well worth paying to go inside the castle, if only to walk along the ramparts and enjoy the commanding views up and down the River Vienne and over the town below. Then you can climb up to the formidable Coudray Tower where some Knights Templar were imprisoned in 1302 before being burnt at the stake. There are also two small museums inside, neither of which are particularly inspiring. One is dedicated to Joan of Arc; the other in the *Logis Royal* (royal quarters) does little more than chart the history of the château by means of a few diagrams and family trees.

Château de Chinon. Tel: 47 93 13 45
Opening times: Feb-Nov 9am-noon and 2-5pm; closed Wednes Feb-Mar and Sept-Nov
Admission: 12F

The **Musée Animé du Vin et de la Tonnellerie**, on the corner of Place de l'Hôtel de Ville, is fun. You are taken through the history of vine cultivation, wine making and cooperage by means of animated life-sized figures going about their traditional crafts in life-like sets complete with realistic sound effects and a recorded commentary in French. The machinery which makes the cooper start hammering, the cellarman draw wine from a barrel and so on, is very cleverly conceived and will keep children amused while parents finish off the tour with a tasting of the real stuff.

Opening times: daily, except Thurs, Apr-Sept
Admission: 12F

The main street of old Chinon, **Rue Voltaire**, is a classic mediaeval road, paved with flagstones and cobbles and overhung with tall, timber-framed houses and a few fine stone mansions with ornately carved façades. Good examples of both these types of building are at the Grand Carroi main cross-roads. Some feel that Rue Voltaire has been too perfectly restored for the sake of tourism, and that, in its sanitised form, it has lost character. Certainly, there are countless boutiques cashing in on associations with Joan of Arc, Rabelais and so on. However, it is worth ambling up and down the colourful thoroughfare. Don't miss the Romanesque Church of St. Maurice on the left as you walk away from the Place de l'Hôtel de Ville.

From the Grand Carroi you can take an alternative steep, winding, cobbled and flagstoned street up to the Château. There is an old stone well half-way up, where Joan is said to have stopped for her horse to drink.

One of the great pleasures of Chinon is to sit in **La Place de l'Hôtel de Ville** and sip a pastis or have a snack lunch, ordered from La Panarge café and served at tables in the middle of the square. As well as being in the shadow of the ruined castle, there is something quintessentially French about the square.

There are several *caves* dotted around town, offering free tastings of Chinon wine. One of these, behind the castle, is next to a small vineyard called **Clos de l'Echo** on account of a tradition of standing there and listening to the echo off the castle wall. The custom seems to be for hopeful young men to shout something like this: *'Sont elles fidèles? les femmes de Chinon'*. To which the castle's echo replies reassuringly *'elles?...non'*.

✪ FONTEVRAUD ABBEY

Don't hurry Fontevraud Abbey. As central to English history as it is to French, the abbey comprises one of the most extensive collections of mediaeval monastic buildings in Europe. Surprisingly, it is at the heart of a delightful, small and not overly touristy town of narrow streets lined with potted plants, with a serene, villagey atmosphere.

The abbey buildings are glaringly white, and bejewelled with stained glass windows. Founded in 1099, it flourished under the royal favour it found with the Plantagenets and at one time included five separate communities (monks, nuns, 'fallen women', lepers and invalids) all living in isolation from each other – you can visit their separate cloisters, kitchens and refectories.

There are also acres of courtyards and mediaeval gardens to wander around. However, the highlight, in terms of historical significance and the reverential aura which goes with it, is the crypt where four Plantagenets lie entombed. Effigies in intricately carved tufa stone show King Henry II of England peacefully asleep; his wife, Eleanor of Aquitaine, is holding a book; their son, Richard the Lionheart, looks stern and authoritative with one hand on his staff; and Isabelle of Angoulême (daughter of King John) shows a little-girl-lost sort of expression.

Fontevraud Abbey

The cavernous 12th-century abbey church itself is a stupendous building with soaring columns, a triple apse and long ambulatory. If you're lucky enough to have it to yourself for a moment, it is worth stopping and listening to the haunting, history-packed silence of the empty church. The same sort of ethereal atmosphere can be experienced daily at 4pm, when a short recital of Latin Gregorian Plainchant echoes around the stone vastness.

There are two other features within the abbey grounds which should not be missed. One is the octagonal monastic kitchen with its giant hearths and chimneys where meat and fish were smoked. It will look familiar to anybody who has visited Glastonbury Abbey. Finally, leave time to see St Mary's cloisters with their beautiful Renaissance vaulting and tiled floor, set around a cool courtyard.

Fontevraud l'Abbaye. Tel: 41 51 71 41
Opening times: all year 9am-7pm
Admission: adult 25F; child 6F

Tucked away on a backstreet, outside the abbey grounds, is the delightful little **St Michel Church** with beautiful lighting and recorded music playing. Its intimate atmosphere contrasts strikingly with the majestic proportions of the abbey. It is also a refreshingly cool retreat in summer.

☆ THE MUSHROOM MUSEUM

The Musée du Champignon is much more fun than it might sound. It is housed entirely underground in a long series of inter-connecting caves under the white cliffs which rise up from the Loire. An English guide will be provided for groups of four people or more. Otherwise it's either a tour in French, or wandering around by yourself with an explanatory English leaflet. In fact, the latter is so clear that it is probably preferable to the 45-minute tour.

You half expect the exhibits to be stalacmites and stalactites as you walk through an entrance cut into the cliff wall. It's dank and gloomy inside with subdued lighting which contrasts the brilliant white of some of the walls with passages leading off into blackness. In places, access from one cave to another is lower than shoulder height.

The caves themselves are intriguing. They are studded with marine fossils, demonstrating how this whole area was once under the sea. Great rectangular blocks have been quarried out of the walls; it is even said that some of the stone used to build Westminster Abbey came from here.

The mushrooms are grown in cavities left by the quarrying. You can see the whole process of mushroom farming: the preparation

The Mushroom Museum, 'La Houssaye'

of the compost; incubation; *gobetage* when peat and crushed rock are tipped onto the trays to promote growth; and finally the harvesting. Apparently over 120,000 tonnes of mushrooms a year are grown in the caves around this area. A very educational hour.

Le Musée du Champignon, 'La Houssaye', signposted from the D751 west of St Hilaire-St Florent. Tel: 41 50 31 55
Opening times: daily 10am–7pm Mar 15–Nov 15
Admission: adult 28F; child 16F

☆ # RICHELIEU

This curious little town is worth a detour. The great 17th-century despot Cardinal Richelieu planned it himself, hoping to make it one of the finest cities in France. A glance at the town map shows that it is as symmetrical as a chess board, with a gateway in the middle of each of its four straight flanks. The broad streets make up an almost perfect grid and in the middle is a large, open square. Look out for the covered, oak-beamed market place at the edge of the square.

The southern gateway leads into a large park of straight avenues lined with huge chestnut trees, formal gardens, domed pavilions, arbours, ornamental lakes and bridges. The Cardinal would have been happy with the great sense of splendour, although the relentless symmetry of everything is disconcertingly unnatural. The park was once the grounds of an ostentatious château which Richelieu built for himself using, among other materials, some of the stones from Chinon's château. Fittingly, some feel, Richelieu's château was confiscated by the French Crown after his death, demolished, and sold as building material. Hardly a trace of it remains.

Today the town is an important agricultural centre. Market days are Saturday and Monday.

Richelieu: 'Les Halles' covered market

ST HILAIRE-ST FLORENT WINE-TASTING

Sweet and dry still whites as well as reds of various descriptions are grown in the gently rolling, chalky vineyards which cover the land south of Saumur. However, it is the crisp, fresh, bone-dry sparkling wines, made from the Chenin Blanc grape which thrives in the limestone soil, for which the region is best known. The caves on the banks of the Loire, whether natural or cut into the tufa cliffs, provide the much-needed cool conditions for the long, complicated *Méthode Champenoise* by which the wine is made.

St Hilaire-St Florent, just west of Saumur on the D751, is where most of the *caves* are and the place to go to learn all about the method and taste the final product. Many of the producers provide guided tours of their underground *caves*, as well as tastings and varying degrees of pressure to buy. The biggest company is **Ackerman-Laurance**, its name emblazoned all over the town.

Much is made of the fact that the company's founder, Jean Ackerman, brought the Champagne method to the Loire in 1811. Guided tours (you may be lucky enough to get an English-speaking guide, but don't count on it) take you through the entire process from cultivating the vines, harvesting and pressing the grapes, to the all-important Champagne method itself which can be seen in operation.

Saumur vineyard in autumn

Remuage of bottles of Saumur wine

The young wine is bottled with yeasts added to cause a secondary fermentation; then comes the extraordinary *remuage*, whereby the bottles are stored in racks with their necks tilted downwards, while every day for months each one is manually twisted and the tilt increased a fraction until the sediment is all in the neck of the up-turned bottle. The next process is *dégorgement* when the neck is dipped into a freezing solution, the little block of icy sediment removed as if by surgery and replaced with a tiny quantity of liqueur to give it extra character. Then the final cork is inserted and wired.

For those interested enough to concentrate on what is going on, the tour at Ackerman-Laurance, or a similar one at the **Gratien et Meyer** cellars to the east of Saumur on the D947 towards Chinon, is fascinating. For simply tasting, especially if you are looking for something to buy, there are countless other producers inviting you to a free *dégustation*.

Ackerman-Laurance, St Hilaire-St Florent. Tel: 41 50 25 33
Opening times: Easter-Sept 1 9.30am-5.30pm; rest of year 9am-noon and 3-5.30pm
Gratien et Meyer, Château de Beaulieu, Route de Montsoreau. Tel: 41 51 01 54
Opening times: all year 9-11.30am and 2-5.30pm

Just south of Saumur and St Hilaire-St Florent, in the village of Bagneux, is one of the largest and most impressive of the thousands of neolithic **dolmens** which dot France. This one is a long, flat, stone structure which was originally a burial chamber. Strangely, it is in the garden of a café. It is signposted from the D147 out of Saumur. Admission: 6F.

☆ SAUMUR

Saumur used to be among the most important towns of the Loire. During the 16th and 17th centuries it was a commercial hub, principal port, and one of the main centres in France for Protestantism. Today, its population of about 35,000 is less than it was 400 years ago. The strikingly white château, perched on a clifftop overlooking the town, stands in dramatic testimony to this illustrious past.

The Edict of Nantes, which guaranteed freedom of worship in France, was revoked in 1685. This led to persecution of the

The dolmen at Bagneux

Protestants, who fled in great numbers. Commercial activity collapsed in their wake, and the city never recovered. A century and a half later the railways came, and that was the end of Saumur as a port. Today it is a compact, rather lovely little place with a busy, small-town atmosphere. It is well worth wandering around for a few hours.

Parking is relatively easy in Saumur. You may well be able to find a place along the waterfront or on the Ile d'Offard opposite the main part of the town. Walking across the Pont Cassart is a fine introduction; the disproportionately large **Tourist Office**, complete with piles of literature and mini wine and mushroom exhibitions, is straight in front of you at the end of the bridge.

Tufa stone becomes whiter as it ages and the massive **Château de Saumur**, crowned with turrets pointing skywards, was built in the 14th century from some of the purest of the local soft, chalky rock. No wonder it looks like a cross between a fairy-tale castle and a wedding cake.

Since the château is visible from everywhere in the town, finding it is less of a problem than the steep, winding climb up can be for the unfit. Before going in, it is worth strolling around the beautifully kept gardens which surround the château, and looking out over the stone balustrade at wonderful views up and down the Loire and over endless, gently rolling farmland and vineyards on the other side of the river.

Wander the gardens at leisure, because once you've climbed the worn, cobbled walkway up to the château's entrance, you may find that the guides are running a rather dictatorial régime within the portals. Inside, these guides rattle on (in French, with English leaflets) through the scores of exhibits and the history of Saumur, while keeping their parties moving as if they were in a prison exercise yard.

Nevertheless, the hour-long tour is worth taking. Rather than the endless collection of furniture, fine art, tapestries and armour familiar to the regular château visitor, this château has been turned into two separate museums. The first is the **Musée du Cheval** which charts the history of the horse as a domesticated animal, illustrated by a huge collection of saddles, stirrups, spurs and other bits and pieces which are lost on the non-equestrian but may be of great interest to the more horsey visitor. Saumur's cavalry school and its prominence in thoroughbred breeding are

Tufa cliffs and troglodyte village near Saumur

also explained in their historical contexts. The strangest exhibit is the skeleton of an English horse called Flying Fox which, as all good racing historians will recall, won the Derby, the Two Thousand Guineas and the St Leger Stakes in 1899.

The other museum is the **Musée d'Arts Décoratifs**. Along with the furniture, paintings and tapestries is an extensive collection

The town of Saumur, overlooked by its Château

of exquisite Limoges porcelain. Some marble and carved wood statuettes are also worth a look.

The large old iron key just inside one of the entrances, pointed out to all visitors, is unremarkable except for the fact that a US soldier stole it as a memento during the first world war. In 1964 the old man appeared in the town with the thing, confessing that he had suffered years of guilt. A ceremony was then held, at which he was officially pardoned amid the popping of sparkling Saumur corks.

Château de Saumur. Tel: 41 51 30 46
Opening times: daily Jul–Sept 15 9am–7pm; Sept 15–end June 9am-noon and
2-5.30pm, closed Tues
Admission: adult 28F; child 10F

A WALK AROUND SAUMUR

Saumur is small and compact enough to make it easy to absorb most points of interest in a few hours' walk around the town. Starting at the Château, wind through the tightly clustered old town, down to the river where several tall, quaintly distorted original timber-framed houses are scattered among more recent erections in white tufa stone. The Romanesque **Church of St Pierre** is worth a look, especially the entrance which fans out into a series of concentric archways to create a tunnel effect.

To the right is **Montée du Fort** – a dark, narrow alley said to be the one Balzac had in mind when he wrote *Eugénie Grandet*, his study of miserliness which is possibly the most depressing novel ever written. The author described this backstreet in terms symbolic of the misery which went on behind the Grandet front door. These days it is still dark and overshadowed, but rather quaint and attractive with it.

Behind the church is the more cheerful main riverside road. Cross over and walk along the Quai Mayaud waterfront where windsurfers, canoeists and swimmers mess about in the water. On Saturday, an open-air food market is held on the quayside. To the left just before you reach the bridge is the **Maison de Ville**, the town hall, its splendid transitional Gothic-Renaissance style recalling some of the former grandeur of Saumur.

Straight avenues lined with elegant shops and broad pavements colonised by café terraces characterise most of modern Saumur. Before leaving the town, it is worth stretching your legs down one of these streets in order to gain a sense of how successfully a modern town can co-exist comfortably, and aesthetically, with its mediaeval quarter. The Château is rarely out of sight, so finding your way back to the starting point is no problem.

On the Rue Franklin Roosevelt in modern Saumur is a cute little *pâtisserie*, **La Duchesse Anne**, with a few tables where you can sit and taste a wonderful selection of chocolate delicacies crafted in all kinds of animal shapes. Small children go wild over them, providing adults with an excuse to gorge themselves.

☆ VIENNE VALLEY DRIVE

While an officially designated and signposted *Route Touristique du Val de Vienne* plots a course through the countryside south of the tributary, there is an exceptionally pretty, lesser-used route along the north bank. This is the D8. Starting at sleepy little L'Ile-Bouchard and its island in the Vienne, take the road towards Chinon. Weeping willows droop down to the water's edge as a sea of rolling vineyards opens out to the right.

Cabernet Franc is the grape varity grown here. It produces dry, earthy wines of which the red Chinons of this area are among the most characterful. Oz Clarke has described them as '...quite delicious, so long as you're the kind of person who takes kindly to cold showers and no sugar in your tea'. At Chezelet there are several *caves* open to the public, including 'Domaine de

Chezelet', on the right just beyond the village. The rustic, hearty *vigneron*, Jacques Gasnier, lines up his various *cuvées* with pride. There are several more *caves* between here and Briançon, as you wind along the river bank, occasionally veering inland through vineyards interspersed with fields of bright yellow sunflowers standing in regimented rows or hay harvested into neat rectangles looking like giant flapjacks.

Then comes one of the great moments in touring the Loire. You unexpectedly round a corner to meet the awesome sight of cliff-hanging Chinon, crowned by the jagged towers of its ruined Château.

Just on the Ile-Bouchard side of the village of Briançon, you can drive down a track to the edge of the River Vienne and a beautiful grassy **picnic spot** where your only company is likely to be the odd fisherman hunched on the bank, or sitting in a wooden rowing boat. This is also a lovely place to take a stroll along the tow-path.

Fields of sunflowers in the Vienne Valley

WHERE TO STAY

Chênehutte-les-Tuffeaux
🏠 ✕ 🛏 *££££*

Le Prieuré, *Chênehutte-les-Tuffeaux, F-49350 Gennes*
Tel: 41 67 90 14
Closed Jan-early Mar
A wonderful converted mediaeval priory with sweeping views up and down a wide stretch of the Loire from the dining room and some of the bedrooms. There are exquisite antiques throughout, and every room is decorated in a different, tasteful style. There is a heated outdoor swimming pool and a tennis court. The modern, imaginative and well-presented cooking contrasts with the old-world style of the building. Last orders: lunch 2pm; dinner 9.30pm.

Chinon
🏠 ✕ 🛏 *££*

La Boule d'Or, *66, quai Jeanne-d'Arc, F-37500 Chinon*
Tel: 47 93 0313
H closed Dec 15-Jan 30
R closed Sun eve and Mon Oct - mid-Apr
A friendly little *Logis de France* down by the river, with just the quayside road between the front-facing rooms and views across the Vienne. The rooms at the back are quieter and look onto a courtyard. The simple, good-value restaurant gives onto a backstreet off the lively Rue Voltaire - the pedestrianised main thoroughfare of Chinon. Last orders: lunch 2pm; dinner 9pm.

Montsoreau
🏠 ✕ 🛏 *££*

Le Bussy, *F-49730 Montsoreau*
Tel: 41 51 70 18
H closed Dec 15-Jan 31
R closed Mon and Tues lunch
A highly recommended little hotel in a converted old house, with the white tufa cliff forming one wall. Outside are terraced gardens with views over the Loire and Montsoreau castle. Bedrooms are comfortable, with a rustic feel to them. The restaurant, called **Diane de Meridor**, is housed separately, about 200 yards away in the lower part of the village. There are great views over the river, even for those with their backs to the window, as the wall opposite is entirely mirrored. Delicious home cooking, with plenty of river fish on the menu. Last orders: lunch 2pm; dinner 9pm.

Richelieu
🏠 ✕ 🛏 *£*

Hôtel Le Puits Doré, *Place du Marché, F-37120 Richelieu*
Tel: 47 58 10 59
Closed Sat Oct-Mar
Behind an unpromising, somewhat dilapidated exterior on the town's main square, is this cosy, smartly decorated and extremely friendly little hotel offering excellent value for money. Some rooms have baths, others just showers; all are comfortable and well equipped. The restaurant is a bargain and is particularly popular with locals. Last orders: lunch 2pm; dinner 9pm.

Saumur
🏠 🛏 ££

Anne d'Anjou, *32, quai Mayaud, Saumur*
Tel: 41 67 30 30
Closed 2 wks Christmas
A delightful hotel with large, tastefully decorated rooms which have views either of the River Loire or of the Château. Extremely good value. Recent visitors, according to the proprietor, include Monsieur Terry Wogan, and the British Ambassador to France. There are also four very grand suites, all overlooking the river. Even these are quite reasonably priced. In the garden behind is Les Ménestrels restaurant (see Where to Eat).

Saumur
🏠 ✕ 🛏 ££

Loire Hôtel, *Rue du Vieux Pont, F-49400 Saumur*
Tel: 41 67 22 42
Open all year
A modern hotel build in traditional style on the Ile d'Offard, with magnificent views over the river and the château-crowned main part of the town. The rooms are comfortable, well equipped and tastefully decorated. The restaurant, **Les Mariniers**, specialises in fish dishes. There is also a huge selection of cheeses. Book in advance to get a table with a river view. Last orders: lunch 2pm; dinner 9.30pm.

WHERE TO EAT

Chinon
✕ 🛏 £££

Au Plaisir Gourmand, *2, rue Parmentier, Chinon*
Tel: 47 93 20 48
Closed Sun eve and Mon; Feb and 2 wks Nov
Sip an *apéritif* on the wisteria-draped terrace of this secluded old house off a back street in old Chinon. Then take your place in the exclusive little dining room where some of the best cooking in the region is served. The food is elaborate, though not pretentiously so. Palate-refreshing sorbets are served between courses. If you really want to sample the best on offer, go for the *Menu à Dégustation*, seven small courses. It is essential to book in advance as this tiny little place has become one of the most popular restaurants in the area. Last orders: lunch 1.30pm; dinner 9pm.

Fontevraud
✕ 🛏 £££

La Licorne, *Allée St Catherine, Fontevraud-l'Abbaye*
Tel: 41 51 72 49
Closed Sun eve and Mon
This is a truly classy place on a charming, narrow alley behind St Michel church. There are a few tables in the front garden, which becomes particularly beautiful in the evening with the help of clever lighting. Inside the 18th-century stone house there are only a handful more tables, making it a very select place. The food has gained an outstanding reputation locally, and you'd be advised to book well in advance. Last orders: lunch 1.15pm; dinner 8.45pm.

L'Ile-Bouchard

✗ ▭ ££

Auberge de l'Ile, *3, place Bouchard, l'Ile Bouchard*
Tel: 47 58 51 07
Closed Sun eve, Mon, and all Feb
A discreet little restaurant on an island in the middle of the River Vienne, near some of the best *caves* offering tastings of Chinon wine. In summer you can sit outside on a terrace overlooking a stretch of water popular with anglers. The menu is extensive with wholesome, regional fare served in large portions, as well as lighter, *nouvelle cuisine*-ish dishes. Last orders: lunch 2pm; dinner 9pm.

Saumur

✗ ▭ ££

Les Ménestrels, *11, rue Raspail, Saumur*
Tel: 41 67 71 10
Closed Sun, Mon lunch and Jan 15-30
A very elegant restaurant in a bright, airy converted barn in the garden of Hôtel Anne d'Anjou. The cooking is in a modern style with lightly sauced dishes, attractively presented, and supplemented by an excellent wine list including many of the best of the lesser-known local wines, such as earthy red Saumur-Champigny. Last orders: lunch 2pm; dinner 9.30pm.

GREGORIAN PLAINCHANT

Few people who have visited a monastery and witnessed the community of monks coming together to sing their Divine Offices in Gregorian Plainchant can have failed to be moved by the experience. Benedictine monasteries the world over still use this unaccompanied line of flowing melody, the rhythms varying with the words, to sing psalms and other parts of their liturgy. They have maintained the tradition because of the very simple spirituality and emotion which it expresses.

Plainchant is generally accepted as being the earliest form of Western music and a cornerstone on which European classical music was built. The simple melodies to which the early Christians sang their daily prayers were first codified in the 6th century under Pope Gregory I (the one who sent St Augustine to evangelise Britain) by adapting the Greek system of using letters to represent notes - hence the origins of our present notation for reading and writing music.

Solesmes Abbey is one of the greatest places in the world for listening to plainchant; other places in the Loire Valley where you can take a break from the outside world to listen to this ethereal music include the Abbeys of Fontevraud and St Benoît.

INDRE VALLEY
AND BOURGUEIL

Most people who have explored the Indre agree that it is among the loveliest of the Loire's many tributaries. Some may find the nuclear power station at its mouth to be an unpromising start, but a little way up are two of the most enchanting châteaux in the entire Loire valley: Ussé, with its special appeal for young children; and Azay-le-Rideau, a jewel of the French Renaissance.

As you drive along the Indre through peaceful, secluded countryside, there are plenty of opportunities to get out and stretch your legs on the waterside paths, or by turning off into the Forest of Chinon. A short detour also takes the literary minded to Saché, where a minor château has become a museum to Balzac, who wrote several of his novels there. Nearby is Villaines-les-Rochers where you can see the village's famous wicker-workers at their craft.

Deeper into Touraine, on the south bank of the River Cher, lies Villandry, a château whose formal gardens are unmissable for anyone with even a passing interest in horticulture. Nor should anybody with even faintly vinous tendencies bypass the town of Bourgueil, north of the Loire, around which some of the most characterful red wine in the region is grown.

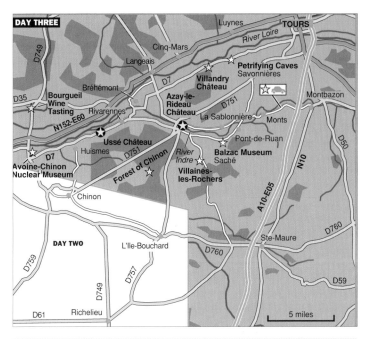

AVOINE-CHINON NUCLEAR MUSEUM

There is something very obviously incongruous about a nuclear power station existing right at the heart of historic château country. It stands at the mouth of the Indre and came on stream in 1963 as France's first commercial, electricity-generating nuclear plant. Ever since then, it has aroused passions on both side of the nuclear debate.

There is nothing discreet or apologetic about the station. Its huge silver sphere and billowing white water vapour are unmistakable landmarks for miles around, from both banks of the Loire. It seems simultaneously suggestive of a James Bond-ish science fiction and a mediaeval fairy tale. As you cross the Loire, the reality of quite how vast the silver ball is becomes apparent. You might also note the scores of anglers dangling their rods from the bridge: fish apparently thrive on the warm effluent!

The visitors' entrance is just by the Port-Boulet bridge, and the tour of the redundant Chinon A complex (Chinon B next to it is still a 'live' reactor) takes about 1½ hours. You have to be very technically-minded really to understand what is going on, but children seem to be in awe of the control room, the sealed air-lock you have to pass through to reach a domed interior, the huge pipes and the space-age lift which whisks you high up to the top of the building. From here there are expansive views over the surrounding area, but, sealed away from the world, it feels more like watching a film.

Centrale Nucléaire d'Avoine-Chinon, Avoine. Tel: 47 98 77 77
Opening times: tours at 9 and 10.30am, 2 and 3.30pm. You should confirm by tele-phone that you are coming and bring some identification
Admission free

 ## AZAY-LE-RIDEAU CHATEAU

Descriptions of this perfectly proportioned Renaissance building usually end up as strings of lyrical superlatives. Balzac called it a 'cut diamond set in the Indre'. Even the most expectant are staggered by its graceful beauty as they stand in front of its façade, mirrored in the moat. Perhaps only the Taj Mahal has the same capacity to surpass expectations of perfection.

Château d'Azay-le-Rideau

It was built under the guidance of Philippa Lesbahy, wife of the wealthy royal financier Giles Berthelot, between 1518 and 1529. She saw it as a celebration and culmination of the architectural revolution which the Renaissance had brought to France. Gone is any semblance of the aggression or warlike intimidation characteristic of châteaux which were genuine fortresses with defensive purposes, such as Anjou or Chinon. Instead, turrets, moats and sentry walks are reduced to ornaments, harmonising with the work of art which is the building's overt purpose.

The leafy, lawned grounds surrounding the gleaming white L-shaped château allow you to appreciate its glory to the full. In place of the straight lines and geometric shapes found in so many French gardens, here we have a more rambling, natural effect into which the building blends. The River Indre has been skilfully diverted to surround the château with water; wooden boats, as superfluous to aquatic transport as the turrets are to defence, are moored to the bank.

The interior, it must be said, does not offer quite the same enchantment. There are rare pieces of furniture, fine art and tapestries to be seen in much the same way as in dozens of other Loire châteaux. For those genuinely interested in the minutiae, there are 45-minute guided tours; but, happily, you can also wander around at your leisure, reading descriptions of whatever you find interesting from wall-mounted plaques if your French is good enough. The sumptuous bedrooms with vast fireplaces and carved four-poster beds are worth seeing; so is the great kitchen with its collection of massive pots, pans and utensils. There is also a four-storey Grand Staircase which is very unusual for its era.

Azay-le-Rideau stages one of the most polished *son et lumière* shows in the Loire valley. From the moat-side lawn, spectators watch its history brought dramatically to life, with harsh, almost violently bright lighting giving way to dulcet, soft colours analogous to the Renaissance age.

Château d'Azay-le-Rideau. Tel: 47 45 42 04
Opening times: daily all year except Jan 1, May 1 and Nov 11: Easter-Aug 9.30am-
7pm; Sept 9.30am-6pm; Oct-Easter 9.30am-noon and 2-5.30pm
Admission: adult 25F, child 6F
Son et lumière shows: Easter and every evening from last weekend of May-third week-
end of Sept. Show starts at 10pm and lasts 1 hour
Admission: 50F

The **Café Salamandre** opposite the château entrance is a good place for a snack lunch. The *Croques Monsieur* are made with delicious local cold meats. There is also a delectable selection of custard pastries and glazed fruit tartlets.

BALZAC MUSEUM

The village of Saché is a pretty place set above the River Indre, over which there are glimpses from the grand old 18th-century mansion known as Château de Saché. Inside is the *Musée Balzac* – a house full of memorabilia which the great author's aficionados pour over with reverence and attention to the minutest detail.

Balzac is the Dickens of France, but more so. Some of the most powerful characters in his bitter-sweet *comédie humaine*, such as the tragic Père Goriot and the arch-miser Monsieur Grandet, have made a lasting impression on the French psyche. Honoré de Balzac himself led as colourful a life as his most flamboyant character: he had scores of mistresses, ran up huge debts, and sometimes worked up to 18 hours a day at his furious writing. For months at a time he used to elude his creditors, and escape the petty restrictions of the bourgeois society first in Tours and then Paris, which he so despised. A friend of his, Madame de Margonne, owned Château de Saché at the time, and welcomed him for as long as he wished to stay. Consequently, it became one of his principal homes and was where he wrote some of his greatest novels.

Frankly, you should visit the museum only if details of Balzac's life interest you, and if you can read French. There are rooms full of original manuscripts; his desk, quill pens and other personal effects; and portraits of his ample, mustachioed self and several of his mistresses. All the wall-mounted explanations are in French only, as is the 'Life of Balzac' audio-visual show.

One other point of interest in the village is a curious and rather incongruous iron structure in the main square, the work of a contemporary American sculptor who settled in Saché.

Musée Balzac, Château de Saché, Saché. Tel: 47 26 86 50
Opening times: daily 9.30am-6.30pm; closed Dec and Feb
Admission: adult 20F; child 13F

Bust of the writer Balzac,
Château de Saché

Ripening grapes in a Bourgueil
vineyard

BOURGUEIL WINE-TASTING

Along with Chinon wines, the reds of Bourgueil and St Nicholas-de-Bourgueil are generally considered to be the finest in the Loire. However, rather than heading straight for the two villages themselves, an excellent introduction to these light, delicate wines is to meander through the rural lanes between the farms whose life-blood is the growing of grapes.

Cross to the north bank of the Loire on the D749, leaving the silver ball of the Avoine-Chinon nuclear power station behind you. In just less than three kilometres, the village of La Taille is signposted off to the left. Take this track, which plunges into a world of vineyards, divided into the neat little patches of different smallholdings. La Taille turns out to be just a few farmhouses, with a hand-painted sign hanging outside each one advertising the *vigneron*'s name and offering *dégustations*. Look for the farmer or his wife; if they're not around, try the next farm. In any of them, you are likely to be taken into a cellar or shed and be given some of the local *vin de table* to taste, plus a few different vintages and *cuvées* of Bourgueil or St Nicholas-de-Bourgueil.

After charming, earthy hand-shakes *vignerons* proudly pour their good, bad or indifferent wines as if they were nectar. Be warned: it is almost impossible not to make a purchase from each one you visit.

Le Plessis, Port-Guyet and La Villatte are hamlets of a few farm-houses each. St Nicholas is a larger, attractive little village. But if you are seriously interested in getting to grips with this style of wine, the place to go is to **Maison Audebert et Fils** in Bourgueil itself. Here an English-speaking guide shows you the cellars and can explain how the Cabernet Franc grape, a relative of the Bordeaux Cabernet Sauvignon, was brought to the area, thriving in combination with local soil and climatic conditions to produce a highly singular style of wine.

Maison Audebert et Fils, Avenue Jean Causeret, Bourgueil. Tel: 47 97 70 06
Opening times: daily all year 8am-noon and 2-6pm

Two kilometres north of Bourgueil is the *Moulin Bleu* – a small, painstakingly restored windmill built, fittingly, over a wine cellar. It was once used for grinding the bark of chestnut trees to make leather dye. (Bourgueil was once as famous for its tanneries as for its wine.) From the windmill, there are good views over the vineyards.

☆
THE FOREST OF CHINON

Between two tributaries of the Loire – the Vienne and the Indre – is an ancient hunting forest of oak, pine, cedar and silver birch trees, carpeted with dense bracken. The dead-straight, 20-kilometre-long D751 between Chinon and Azay-le-Rideau slices through the forest. Another road leads south to L'Ile Bouchard. However, on either side of it are large tracts of forest which have been requisitioned by the military: you have to pass through checkpoints and may not leave your car.

For any real appreciation of the *Forêt de Chinon*, you need to get away from the main roads and follow some of the many tracks off into the boscage. One of these leads to St Benoît-la-Forêt (which can also be reached along a winding little forest road from Vigny d'Ussé) where a few cottages are huddled together. This is a good base from which to walk through the woods and enjoy the natural history. Being nocturnal, the foraging wild boar are rarely seen, but you may spot a pair of antlers retreating into the undergrowth as a deer shies away from human intrusion. In summer, balmy breezes waft through the trees, which are alive with birdsong.

The forest is carefully managed, and not exactly wild; rather, it is a nature reserve and popular hunting park. Unmarked trails lead through the woods from clearing to clearing where firewood is gathered into neat bundles. You also come across the occasional isolated cottage, surrounded by a few vegetable patches. There are even one or two tiny vineyards.

Come the autumn, however, constant volleys of shotgun fire reverberate through the trees, and walkers should proceed with care.

☆ ## INDRE DRIVE

The Indre splinters into a delta of islands, marshes and streams as it joins the Loire. It is a minor tributary, and also one of the less explored, despite having two splendid châteaux – Azay-le-Rideau and Ussé – on its lower reaches. A drive from its mouth along the D17 to Montbazon combines these and other architectural and historic wonders with some glorious, secluded countryside crossed by the river, its banks lined with weeping willows, avenues of poplars and water mills fuelled by rushing weirs. In *Le Lys dans la Vallée*, Balzac described the '...lines of poplars guarding this vale of love. A long ribbon of water streaming in the sun between two green banks'. It is easy to see what moved him to such poesy.

Leaving behind the bizarre silver sphere of Avoine-Chinon nuclear power station, the road passes Château d'Ussé, which soon disappears into the forest, and meanders along the riverside. Tracks lead off the road to the left, over wooden bridges spanning channels of the splintered river or irrigation ditches feeding barley fields, strawberry beds and extravagant yellow expanses of sunflowers.

At Quincay, leave the D7 which crosses the Indre to head for Tours, and take the right fork along a quieter road through Armentières and on to Azay-le-Rideau. Here it is worth crossing to the north bank and following the narrow, little-used D84 up to the delightful little hamlet of La Sablonnière, opposite Saché. From here onwards, the Balzac associations are relentless – every village seems to have at least one Café, Rue or Place Balzac; there's even a Balzac fishing tackle shop.

Pont-de-Ruan, a little further upstream, has a pretty stone water mill on an island in the Indre. The valley here feels the most secluded; in places, the banks are entirely canopied with trees and anglers in green jackets huddle in little boats among the reeds. Occasionally one of them will net and land an enormous carp, looking ridiculously out of proportion to the narrow river.

> For an idyllic **picnic spot**, park in Pont-de-Ruan and walk for a couple of hundred yards downstream on the north bank. Wooden planks lead over some irrigation ditches to a grassy river bank in the dappled shade of poplar trees.

Soon after the quaint small town of Monts, the tranquillity is liable to be shattered by the low-flying helicopter of one of the rich and famous people who arrive regularly at Château d'Artigny – considered by some to be one of the finest hotels in France. Shortly after passing the estate's expansive grounds, the road snakes under the A10 flyover, where traffic whizzing between Paris and Bordeaux gets a fleeting glimpse of the idyllic river. Then you are on the outskirts of Montbazon. The main point of interest here is the ruined Foulques Nerra keep above the town, from where there are wonderful views up and down the Indre.

THE PETRIFYING CAVES

These are worth stopping at if you're on the road from Villandry to Tours. After going in through an archway carved into the startlingly white rock, the first thing you notice is how cool the interior is – even in the height of summer the temperature rises little above a steady 14°C. The grottoes and underground passages were quarried from the 12th to 14th centuries, but became flooded and were forgotten about until being rediscovered earlier this century.

The peaceful River Indre

Steadily drip...drip...dripping stalactites and hideously glistening limestone contortions point the way down to a second, Dante-esque chamber discovered only in 1947. An exhibition of realistic dinosaurs has been added to the natural phenomena, causing the grotto to resound with the squeals of children as they come face to face with a Tilosaurus or Ichthyostega. There is also a **Museum of Petrification** which shows you how these bizarre formations are created, and has a collection of sculpted limestone slabs.

The caves can become very overcrowded and claustrophobic. This is perhaps why the 45-minute tour ends with an otherwise inexplicable glass of wine for adults. To avoid the crowds, it's best to go early in the morning.

Grottes Pétrificantes, Savonnières. Tel: 47 50 00 09
Opening times: daily Feb–Dec 15, 9am–6pm ; Nov 1-Dec 15 closed Thurs
Admission: adult 21F; child 13F

On a clifftop at the eastern edge of Cinq-Mars-la-Pile on the D152 between Langeais and Luynes is a strange rectangular tower with a pyramid on each corner. It has no known parallel anywhere in the Loire valley and virtually nothing has been discovered about its origins, except that it was probably built during Roman times. Amateur antiquarians should not miss the chance of trying to crack a real enigma which has baffled scores of scholars.

USSE CHATEAU

Château d'Ussé is pure fairy tale. Terraced gardens rise up from the River Indre to this brilliant white castle of turrets, towers and crenellations perched on a cliff at the edge of the Forest of Chinon. Ussé is widely held to be the setting chosen by Charles Perrault when he wrote *Sleeping Beauty*.

Every last drop of theatre is squeezed out of the association in the guided *La Belle au Bois Dormant* tour. A long and narrow staircase climbs up to the parapets above, and threads through a chain of castle rooms, in each of which there is a life-like display of a chapter in the fairy story. The settings are elaborate and the waxworks very detailed, complete with terrifying Wicked Fairy, smarmy Handsome Prince and the alluring Beauty herself. At last, here is a château where the children will squeal with delight rather than yawn at their umpteenth Flemish tapestry or 17th-century chair that afternoon!

Of course, there is also another tour of the Château. It lasts 45 minutes and is both a good and sad one. You follow the treasure-adorned corridors from the Gothic east side of the Château to the elegant Renaissance west wing and learn the real-life story of the Duchess of Duras, the lady of the house whose husband lost his head on the guillotine during the French revolution. She fell in love with the Romantic author and politician Chateaubriand (he is credited with planting the avenue of cedar trees outside the château for her). When he jilted her, she stilled all the clocks in the Château *'so as never to hear struck the hours when you will not return'*. And there's no happy ending.

Just as poignant is the glorious Royal Chamber – the finest room in the Château - where sumptuous accommodation stood permanently prepared for the royal visit. It never came.

Château d'Ussé, Rigny-Ussé. Tel: 47 95 54 05
Opening times: mid-Mar – mid-Nov 9am-noon and 2-7pm. Just outside the château
entrance is a café serving light snacks
Admission: adult 39F, child 19F

Château d'Ussé

VILLAINES-LES-ROCHERS

This troglodyte village, famous throughout France for its wicker-work, is only a short detour for anyone driving along the valley of the Indre, or visiting Azay-le-Rideau, Saché or Villandry. It's well worth the journey to see an extensive exhibition of intricate wickerwork furniture and ornaments of every kind: tables, chairs, beds, sofas, picture-frames, bowls, clothes-models... anything you can think of. The extraordinarily dexterous craftsmen and women can be seen at work, shaping their malleable material into all sorts of intricate designs. Needless to say, examples of all their wares are for sale.

The full process is carefully explained by the craftsmen to anyone who is interested; some speak a little English. The wicker, which is a kind of willow, is grown on the banks of the Indre and harvested during winter, when the plants have reached a pre-determined size, and soaked for several months. Then it is dried, stripped and prepared for crafting at the *Vannerie de Villaines* – the wicker-workers' co-operative which was founded in 1849 by the local priest to keep this traditional craft alive.

Today, the co-operative provides employment for over 80 families. Much of the work goes on in the tufa stone caves around the village, which are also the homes of some troglodytic families.

Also in some connecting caves at the edge of the village is a traditional iron forge, making and selling hand-crafted fire tongs, grates, door knockers and all kinds of other implements and ornaments. Follow signs to *La Ferronnerie*.

Société Coopérative Agricole de Vannerie, Villaines-les-Rochers, near Azay-le-Rideau.
Tel: 47 43 33 03
Opening times: 9am-noon and 2-7pm Mon-Fri, also Sun Apr-Sept
Admission: free

From just north of Villaines-les-Rochers, on the D217, you can pick up a delightful countryside stretch of the clearly signposted GR3 long-distance **footpath**. It joins the Indre riverside D17 about 5km further on.

☆ VILLANDRY CHATEAU

This fine 16th-century Renaissance château stands on the south bank of the Cher, near its confluence with the Loire. It is surrounded on three sides by a moat which is home to shoals of giant carp, some of which have grown to nearly three feet long. The château tour lasts 30 minutes; there are some English-speaking guides. Of particular note are an extraordinary 13th-century *Mudejar* ceiling brought from Toledo in Spain and re-constructed, and the majestic staircase leading up to the picture gallery where there is a Velázquez, a Tintoretto and two Goyas.

The upper balconies look down on incredible formal gardens. It is for these that Villandry is most famous; in fact, in so château-saturated an area, many visitors forsake the interior and just wander around the esplanades, pergolas, arbours and fountains.

Lovers of the English country park, as influenced by Capability Brown, will be in for a shock. Instead of taming nature while at the same time allowing it to keep inherent characteristics such as

The gardens of Château de Villandry

Sleeping Beauty in Château d'Ussé

gentle contours and the occasional bit of controlled rambling, here is a pointedly geometric, immaculately manicured and striking example of nature under the dictatorship of the gardener. It's like the difference between people coming dressed up for a party on the one hand, and presenting themselves in regimented lines for a military parade on the other.

Whether you love them, or feel that they affront nature by putting her in a strait-jacket, these are some of the most spectacular gardens anywhere. They are arranged on three tiers. The lowest is a *jardin potager* where herbs and vegetables are grown in displays of brightly contrasting purple cabbages, orange tomatoes and bright green beans, all perfect sizes and shapes. On the middle level are the *jardins d'amour* with arrangements of heart-shaped herbaceous borders, hedges clipped with geometric precision, and rows of rose bushes standing to attention. The top level is the water garden with walkways round the ornamental lake which feeds the moats and irrigates the rest of the gardens.

Château de Villandry, on the D7 west of Savonnières. Tel: 47 50 02 09
Opening times: garden - daily all year 8.45am-dusk (or 8pm); château - Apr-Sept 9am-6.30pm, Oct 9am-5.30pm. Closed Nov-Mar
Admission: gardens 24F; château 37F

Some of the sweetest and most luscious **honeydew melons** are grown in the market gardens around Langeais on the north bank of the Loire. These are widely available in the town through the summer months, especially on Sunday mornings when market stalls are piled high with them.

WHERE TO STAY

Azay-le-Rideau
🏠 ✕ ▭ ££

Le Grand Monarque, *3, place de la République, F-37190 Azay-le-Rideau*
Tel: 47 45 40 08
H closed mid-Dec - end Jan
R closed Nov - mid-Mar
Probably the most pleasant place to stay in Azay-le-Rideau, so long as you get one of the refurbished modern bedrooms with en suite bathrooms, rather than one of the older rooms which have yet to receive their face-lift. The restaurant is cheerful, traditional and very good value with large portions of homely food. It is very convenient for the Château; if you are going to the *son et lumière* show, they will make an effort to serve your dinner in time for the start. Last orders: lunch 2.30pm; dinner 9.30pm.

Bréhémont
🏠 ✕ ▭ £££

Le Castel de Bray et Monts,
F-37130 Bréhémont
Tel: 47 96 70 47
H closed mid-Dec - mid-Jan
This little hotel's name seems to be a
rather poor pun on that of the Loire-
side village, reached along a narrow,
little-used road crossing several channels of the splintered Indre. It's a
rather fine 18th-century house with
just seven bedrooms, each one individually decorated and furnished,
and strangely reminiscent of an
English country home. There is also a
small, pretty garden. The food is a
treat, with local ingredients used
wherever possible, and Loire wines at
very fair prices. Last orders: lunch
2pm; dinner 9pm.

Luynes
🏠 ✕ ▭ £££

Domaine de Beauvois,
F-37230 Luynes
Tel: 47 55 50 11
Closed mid-Jan - mid-Mar
A sumptuous château in a secluded
backwater 4km north of Luynes, set
in 400 acres of woodland. It overlooks
a quiet lake and the beautiful countryside beyond. There is a heated
outdoor swimming pool, tennis
court, bicycles for the use of guests,
and fishing on the lake. Rooms are
large and stately - some of them even
regal. The only disappointment is
that the dining room doesn't overlook
the water, but the food is delicious -
modern and imaginative. Excellent
wine list. Last orders: lunch 2pm;
dinner 9.15pm.

Montbazon
🏠 ✕ ▭ ££££

Château d'Artigny,
F-37250 Montbazon
Tel: 47 26 24 24
Closed Dec

You might have to take out a special
mortgage to stay a night here.
However, many of those who can
afford it consider this stupendous
white mansion overlooking the Indre
to be among the very best hotels in
France. A long driveway through
dense woods, up from the D17,
emerges in front of its magnificent
classical façade. Inside, there is an
imperial air about everything from
the gilded ceiling and huge glass
chandeliers to the splendid four-
poster beds and spacious marble
bathrooms with gold taps. There are
wonderful views from every bedroom. The food is equally sumptuous,
immaculately presented and expensive. There is a heated out-door
swimming pool, two tennis courts
and a convenient pad for landing
your helicopter. Last order: lunch
2pm; dinner 9.30pm.

WHERE TO EAT

Azay-le-Rideau
✕ ▭ ££

L'Automate Gourmand, *11, rue du Parc, Chapelle-St Blaise*
Tel: 47 45 39 07
Closed Mon eve and Tues
An extraordinary collection of antique toys and playthings kept in cabinets in the dining room has made this little bistro famous. It is a lively, very friendly little place in Chapelle-St Blaise, just across the main bridge over the Indre and within ten minutes' walk of the Château. Simple, unpretentious food is served with a minimum of fuss. Last orders: lunch 2pm; dinner 9.15pm.

Bourgueil
✕ ▭ £

Restaurant Germain,
Rue A Chartier, Bourgueil
Tel: 47 97 72 22
Closed Sun eve and Mon
Wonderful value for money, this is a bright, cheerful little place in the middle of town, adjoining the baker's shop which also belongs to the owner. Large helpings of simple country-style fare are served together with some strong rustic cheeses. It is just what you need to fill you up after a good wine-tasting session. Needless to say, a fine selection of local vintages is also on offer. Booking is essential on Tuesday, which is market day. Last orders: lunch 2pm; dinner 9.30pm.

Monts
✕ ▭ ££

La Résidence, *13, rue du Val d'Indre, Monts*
Tel: 47 26 95 31
Closed Sun eve and Wednes
Delicious food at very reasonable prices. This Indre-side restaurant (not a hotel, despite its name) has a lovely garden where you can have a pre-meal drink in summer before choosing from delicacies such as *terrine de foie de volaille aux raisins*, or *truite à la vapeur et au beurre citron*. Finish off with some soft, creamy local cheese, or a powerful *chèvre*. Last orders: lunch 2pm; dinner 9.30pm.

St Epain-Noyant
✕ ▭ £££

Auberge du Moulin des Roches, *St Epain-Noyant, Ste Maure*
Tel: 47 65 80 47
Closed Nov - mid-Mar and Mon, except June-Aug
This delightful converted 17th-century watermill on the Manse tributary is worth a short detour from the lower Indre valley. The machinery is in perfect working order, and you can sit and watch it in motion while you eat. Alternatively, in summer you can take a table outside on the terrace by the mill pond where there is an open-air grill. Traditional and regional cuisine is served inside; steaks, mixed grills and salads on the terrace. Last orders: lunch 2.30pm; dinner 9.30pm.

WINE-TASTING

The Loire Valley is one of the great wine-growing regions of France. It's not quite up there with Bordeaux, Burgundy and Champagne, but together with the Rhône and Alsace it ranks next. What the Loire does offer is a breadth of wine styles unmatched in any other region. There are the gentle rosés and whites of Anjou; superb dry *méthode champenoise* from Saumur; gutsy reds such as Chinon and Bourgueil alongside more delicate medium or dry whites in Touraine; sweet or sparkling Vouvray; and the superlative Sancerre at the eastern end of the region.

These are just a few of the better known *Appellation Contrôlée* wines in the area. Wherever you go, there are opportunities for tastings - *dégustations* - , whether at a regional *Maison du Vin* run by a consortium of all the producers and merchants within an area, at the headquarters of a major producer, or simply in the cellar of a small farmer. Tasting is nearly always free but is often accompanied by pressure to buy. So, while wine-tasting can be one of the joys of touring the Loire Valley it can also, if you are not careful, lead to embarrassment or unwanted purchases.

Some of the *Maisons du Vin*, such as the one just opposite the Château in Angers, are excellent. Literature and information on the regions and styles are available and you can taste, by way of introduction, a range of carefully chosen examples of local wines. These are labelled anonymously as generic wines of the region, so that the particular producer's identity remains a secret. These places operate rather like tourist offices and you should feel no obligation to buy, unless you want to.

The same is true at the *caves* of large-scale producers such as Ackerman-Laurance in Saumur where you can take an extremely interesting tour of the cellars and learn how the Champagne method works, or Maison Audebert et Fils in Bourgueil where you are offered 'vertical' (different vintages from the same vineyard) and 'horizontal' (wine of the same year from different vineyards) tastings. In cases such as these you may well want to buy some wine, particularly at Audebert where there is a great selection to choose from, but it's really up to you.

However, when you accept the invitation of a small farmer to taste his wine, you have to be more careful. If you are seriously interested in buying a case or two, feel free to have a quick taste of various different *vignerons'* wines in an area before you make your choice; but if you spend half an hour drinking glassesful at your host's expense, he will certainly expect you to buy a few bottles.

TOURS AND
THE LOIR

The river Loir appears at times to be an almost deliberate contrast with its homonym into which it flows (via, briefly, the Sarthe). An exploration of the Loir offers an entirely different range of possibilities. The towns and villages are quiet, with many delightful and historically rich places neither receiving nor expecting many tourists. Major châteaux which have survived the era when the Loir was of great strategic importance, such as Le Lude, are very few; others, like Lavardin and Montoire, are now romantic ruins free of turnstiles, closing times or official guides. The charm of a river walk or picnic is that of secluded peace rather than a dramatic sweep of waterscape and skyline.

Because of these contrasts, the Loir can be a wonderful counterbalance to the grandeur of the Loire. Probably more than any other of the Loire's tributaries, it deserves time and to be taken seriously. It is also best explored when the weather is fine.

Other than wine-tasting in Vouvray (mandatory for wine enthusiasts), there is only one major sight in this area - the city of Tours, a complete contrast to the tranquillity of the Loir.

Tours is sometimes treated as no more than a base for exploring the châteaux, vineyards, villages and backwaters of Touraine. It is also frequently bypassed altogether by visitors, on the grounds

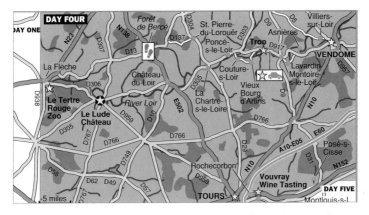

that it is a large, noisy city whose historical monuments have been obliterated. Certainly, its areas of enchantment and historical interest are fewer than say, Blois or Angers. But if you are staying in Tours, there are several sights and museums which it would be a great shame to miss. If your hotel is elsewhere in the region, the imaginatively restored Place Plumereau and St Martin quarter alone fully warrant an incursion into the city centre.

 ## LE LUDE CHATEAU

The small town of Le Lude is rather remote from most itineraries. It is an attractive place on the south bank of the Loir with a beautiful main square, most of the time refreshingly free of tourists. But no *son et lumière* enthusiast should miss it. Dominating the town is the Château where one of the most spectacular of these pageants is performed. The setting is perfect, with the river, fountains, park and the four sturdy towers of the Château exploited to the full. The show itself – entitled 'Sumptuous Nights on the Banks of the Loir' – is an extravagant series of tableaux enacting the Château's history from its time as a defensive stronghold against the English in the Hundred Years War to the era of boudoirs and romantic liaisons in the 19th century. Most amazingly, there is a cast of 350, all in dazzling costumes, acting out the scenes to a background of haunting music and dramatic explosions of colour as fireworks light up the sky.

Château du Lude

In the sobriety of day-light, the Château is rather an odd one. It doesn't seem to have decided quite what to be. The four towers are solid and mediaeval-looking, but are embellished with refinements such as dormer windows and stone carvings; the four walls joining the towers together are as bedecked with windows and ornaments as any stately Renaissance home.

The guided tour of the Château (in French, with an English leaflet) takes about 45 minutes and is the only way to see it. Inside is the familiar collection of furniture, decorations and tapestries. You might find it more refreshing to stroll through the Château's formal gardens, lawns and parkland, which are bisected by the Loir on whose banks the *son et lumière* show is held.

Château du Lude, Le Lude. Tel: 43 94 60 09
Opening times: gardens - daily 9am–noon and 2.30–6pm Apr-Sept; interior - 2–6pm Apr-Sept
The son et lumière (in French) is performed every Friday and Saturday evening at 10pm from June to August, and sometimes additionally on Tuesdays and Thursdays
Admission: house and gardens - adult 22F, child 11F; son et lumière show 45F

> The village of **Vaas**, about half-way along the D305 between Le Lude and Château-du-Loir, has a small sandy beach and is a good place to stop and bathe or hire a rowing boat or pedalo.

FOREST OF BERCE WALK

If you're heading for Le Lude, a lovely diversion from the Loir is to turn right on to the D304 at La Chartre-sur-le-Loir, taking the Le Mans road as far as St Pierre-du-Lorouër, and then turn left to drive through the *Forêt de Bercé*. About 15,000 acres is all that is left of what was once a vast Royal hunting forest, which also supplied some of the finest oak and chestnut wood for centuries of cabinet-making. There are still many magnificent ancient oaks, chestnuts and pines, as well as beeches, sapplings of all kinds and, in places, abundant bracken undergrowth.

Futaie des Clos is as good a place as any to park and walk along the network of trails through carefully forested woods (trees are still felled, discriminately, for furniture-making). You may come across the occasional small herd of fallow deer, well camouflaged in the dappled sunlight.

Follow the D137 through the forest to join the D138 at St Hubert. From here it is a few kilometres down to Château-du-Loir where you can pick up the D305 which follows the Loir to Le Lude.

LOIR VALLEY DRIVE

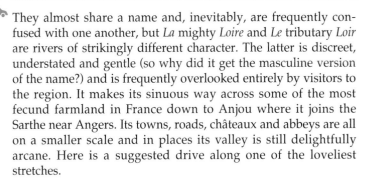

They almost share a name and, inevitably, are frequently confused with one another, but *La* mighty *Loire* and *Le* tributary *Loir* are rivers of strikingly different character. The latter is discreet, understated and gentle (so why did it get the masculine version of the name?) and is frequently overlooked entirely by visitors to the region. It makes its sinuous way across some of the most fecund farmland in France down to Anjou where it joins the Sarthe near Angers. Its towns, roads, châteaux and abbeys are all on a smaller scale and in places its valley is still delightfully arcane. Here is a suggested drive along one of the loveliest stretches.

From Vendôme take the D917 towards Montoire, signposted as *Route Touristique du Val de Loir*. Turn off just beyond Rimay for **Lavardin** with its ruined feudal castle, besieged in 1188 by King Henry II and his son Richard the Lionheart; the castle towers above what is today a sleepy little village. Cross the Loir by a wonderful 12th-century stone bridge and head for **Montoire-sur-**

Ruined castle at Montoire-sur-Loir   *A riverside garden on the Loir*

le-Loir where there is another ruined mediaeval château and some delightful old riverside houses. Don't miss the views up and down the Loir from the bridge. This is another sublimely peaceful place, defying the notoriety it achieved when Hitler and Marshal Pétain met here in 1940.

The straight road from Montoire to Troo is flanked on one side by the Loir, and by numerous troglodyte caves on the other. Here, pick up the *Route Touristique du Val du Loir* again, turning off the D917 which guides you through miles of picture-book farmland and villages such as Vieux Bourg d'Artins, Couture-sur-le-Loir and Manoire de la Possonière, to emerge at **Poncé-sur-le-Loir** where there is a small, private, Renaissance château with formal gardens open to the public. This is also a good place to leave the car and walk along the river bank where fishermen sit crouched in the greenery as the occasional pleasure boat chugs past. Whether you are on foot or wheels, the stretch of the Loir between here and La Chartre-sur-le-Loir is as enchanting as any in the Loire valley.

For a delightful waterside picnic spot with a good chance of being alone, leave the D917 between Vendôme and Montoire, cross to the north bank of the Loir and follow the narrow road which loops round to the hamlet of **Asnières**, following the meandering river. Alongside this lane, there are numerous grassy, shaded spots by the river.

The ancient Forest of Bercé

☆ LE TERTRE-ROUGE ZOO

This isn't as imaginative a zoo as the ones at Doué and Beauval for instance, but the setting in a beautiful wood five kilometres east of La Flèche is wonderful. The collection of mammals is comprehensive - tigers, elephants, monkeys - although their confines are on the small side; also, their cages are huddled together into a corner of the zoo.

The huge aviary is much more worth spending time at, with lots of birds of prey such as eagles and vultures. There is also a large park for ostriches and other flightless birds to run around and bury their heads to escape from the gawping visitors.

The Natural History Museum just opposite the main gates can be visited on the zoo entrance ticket. Hundreds of locally indigenous stuffed animals are displayed in model reconstructions of their habitats, built with extraordinary attention to detail. Explanations are in French and English. In some ways these are more interesting than the live animals.

Parc Zoologique Le Tertre-Rouge, La Flèche. Tel: 43 94 04 55
Opening times: daily 9am-7pm. Closes at dusk Oct-Mar
Admission: adult 45F; child 20F

☆ TOURS

Finding your way into Tours can be an absolute pain. Jungles of industrial sprawl and concrete flyovers encircle the ancient capital of Touraine, spilling over from its central area between the River Loire and its tributary the Cher, a few miles upstream of their confluence. But it's worth making the effort.

The city has countless claims to historical fame. It was a major mediaeval pilgrimage destination with thousands journeying overland to the tomb of St Martin, the great proselytiser who is said to have offered half his cloak to a beggar. In 1461 Louis XI made Tours the capital of France; with the royal presence, the city prospered enormously, becoming a major centre for producing armaments, jewellery and silk fabrics.

When Henri IV moved his court to Paris, Tours' fashionability declined, although it remained one of the most commercially important cities on the Loire. In 1870 it was severely bombarded by the Germans during the Franco-Prussian war; then in 1940 some of the most historic areas of the city were blasted out by the Luftwaffe. In 1944 Tours was heavily bombed again, this time by the Allies trying to cut off German lines of communication. People who remember the city in the early 1960s describe a giant slum of dilapidation and depression.

Since then, Tours has bounced back and its heart has begun to beat again. The city centre, around the Place Plumereau, has been completely and imaginatively restored with surviving original buildings standing side by side with authentic replicas; a new university and international language school have been established, filling the streets and cafés with a youthful vibrancy, and two small, but outstanding, museums have been opened.

Avoid Tuesday for a day-trip into Tours: this is closing day for the museums and several other attractions. The **Tourist Office** is on Place du Mar-Leclerc; tel: 47 05 58 08.

Timber-frame houses on Place Plumereau in Tours

From wherever you've managed to park, follow signs to *La Vieille Ville St Martin*. These signs point the way down narrow, paved, boutique-lined alleys to **Place Plumereau** – a large open square surrounded on four sides by original or reproduction tall timber-frame and red-brick houses. At weekends or on summer evenings, the square is alive with street entertainers surrounded by crowds of laughing or applauding spectators. Students drink beer and strum guitars in large open-air cafés in the centre of the square; people of all ages walk around the fully pedestrianised quarter choosing a restaurant from the countless possibilities, while others simply enjoy a wander through their revitalised city centre.

> If you've had enough of wine-tasting *Le Palais de la Bière* is a bar on Place Gaston-Pailhou where over 250 French and foreign beers are served. There are also nearly 100 single malt and blended whiskies.

It took nearly 400 years to build **St Gatien Cathedral**, starting in the early 13th century. By the time it was completed, architectural tradition in the Loire had been reborn, turning its back on mediaeval notions. Herein lies the fascination of St Gatien – a mélange of styles charting four centuries of architectural evolution. A parallel would be if London's St Paul's cathedral was still being built today, with contemporary features being added.

Perhaps the most surprising thing about St Gatien, (other than the fact that it survived three massive bombardments of the city without losing so much as a pane of its 13th-century stained glass windows), is that somehow an overall harmony is maintained despite the extraordinary diversity of styles. The towers are solid and thick-set; flamboyant carvings have been added to the austere, mediaeval west front; and the 15th-century nave seems perfectly at home with the simpler 13th-century chancel and transept. However, the pride of St Gatien is its windows with shades of red and blue throwing patches of shimmering colour onto the bright, white stone.

Until well into the next century scaffolding is likely to mar the overall aspect of some parts of the cathedral, as the crumbling, blackened exterior and brilliant white tufa stone interior are gradually restored.

The former Archbishop's palace, next to the Cathedral, now houses a **Fine Arts Museum**, including Rembrandt's 'Flight into Egypt', a Rubens, a Dégas and two Mantegnas – all in a rather stuffy atmosphere. There is also a large collection of silk hangings woven in Tours, and rare pieces of furniture which, frankly, are likely to appear as just 'more of the same' to all but the most knowledgeable and dedicated on the château beat. The formal gardens surrounding the fine 17th-century house are shaded by an enormous cedar tree; this can be a peaceful place to escape to for a few minutes, and has a fine view of the cathedral.

Musée des Beaux Arts, 18, place François Sicard. Tel: 47 05 68 73
Opening times: 9am-12.45pm and 2–6pm; closed Tues
Admission: 30F; children free

 What makes the **Touraine Wine Museum** outstanding among the many museums dedicated to promoting the various wine-growing regions along the Loire is the absorbing way in which Touraine's vinous traditions are explained in terms of folklore and social customs. It's all marvellously well done. You can go around alone, or on a guided tour, in French, which takes about 45 minutes. There are explanatory leaflets in English. You descend into the gloomy 12th-century cellars of a monastery, next to the St Julien church. Most of the monastery had been totally destroyed long since, but these cellars were discovered in 1940 after the bombing. With subtle use of lighting and sound effects, the atmosphere of mediaeval secret societies and brother-

Wine brotherhood in Tours

Smart troglodyte home in Troo

hoods which grew up around the mysteries of wine-making is re-created. Amid the aura, it is easy to forget that wine is simply a drink, made from grapes.

Musée de Vins de Touraine, Celliers St Julien, 16, rue Nationale. Tel: 47 61 07 93
Opening times: daily 9am-5.45pm; closed Dec and Jan
Admission: adult 10F; children free

 The **Trade Guild Museum** is housed in the same monastery ruins as the Wine Museum, and is under the same management. It also has a rather similar flavour, tracing the history of many different crafts and the weird rituals which grew up around them. It explains how secret societies were formed to protect common interests and how nationwide and eventually international (in the case of Masons) brotherhoods grew up around them. The effect is a fascinating blend of the evolution of these skills with the extraordinary social history which carried them along.

Musée du Campagnonnage, Cloître St Julien, 8, rue Nationale. Tel: 47 61 07 93
Opening times: daily all year 9am-6pm
Admission: adult 20F; children free

☆   ## TROO

A church crowns Troo's steep conical hill rising, rather like Glastonbury Tor, out of a flat, expansive landscape of wheat fields through which the Loir makes its lazy way.

The village is a terrific place to explore on foot. From the main street, which follows the contours of the hillside, follow signs to *La Butte*, up some stone alleys to the footpath out of the main part of the village, winding up towards the summit. As soon becomes apparent to walkers, as the track snakes past chimney pots and television aerials, the steep tufa-stone hill is itself a sub-urb - a trendy underground one, with rows of troglodyte homes cut into the rock and inhabited by well-to-do families. Clipped privet-hedges and garden gates surround the cave entrances, behind which are the fitted kitchens and bathrooms, antiques and hi-fi systems of the cave dwellers. Some of these are second homes (including several British-owned ones); others are full-time residences.

The view from the top, where there is a small church with a nipple-like belfry standing out for miles around, is spectacular. On a clear day the eye can follow the course of the Loir all the way from Vendôme to La Chartre. From the church a signposted path leads to 'Le Grand Puits'– an immensely deep, wooden-roofed well also known as 'le puits qui parle' on account of the resounding echo as you shout down the shaft. From the well, either retrace your footsteps back to above-ground Troo, or follow the winding road down to the Loir and walk back along the bank.

 ## VENDÔME

A local tourist leaflet describes Vendôme as 'a flowery Venice'. Well...not quite, but the Loir does splinter into several channels as it flows into the town, creating narrow waterways spanned by quaint old stone bridges and lined with twee cottages hung with baskets of geraniums. It is enchanting to wander round, although you do have to penetrate some unsightly industrial suburbs before finding this picturesque kernel.

Vendôme is also rich in historical buildings and associations, most of which can be explored in a short walking tour of the town centre. Start with the **Holy Trinity Abbey**, said to have

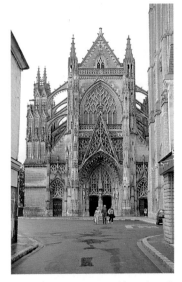
Vendôme: La Trinité abbey church

Narrow waterway with geranium-covered bridge

been founded in 1034 after the Count and Countess of Anjou saw three stars shoot from the sky into the river. The Count ordered a monastery to be built on the site of the miracle, and it became one of the most powerful in Europe with extensive grounds and a glorious church, cloisters and chapter house. However, it was badly damaged during the Wars of Religion and disbanded during the French Revolution, eventually becoming a regional military headquarters. Some surviving parts of the cloisters and chapter house have been restored and you pass through them on the way to a small, rather disparate museum exhibiting relics of stonework salvaged from the monastery, a few mediaeval and Renaissance religious paintings set in Vendôme, and displays of handicrafts.

The museum is open all year from 10am-noon and 2-6pm. Tel: 54 77 26 13
Admission: adult 13F; children free

Only **La Trinité**, the abbey church, survived the various onslaughts unscathed and has a wonderfully flamboyant Gothic façade. Inside, look out for the stunning stained glass window in each of a series of interior chapels, and don't miss the amusing wooden seats carved into sculptures of mediaeval folk with milk pails yoked over their shoulders, at work in their iron forges, or going about their daily business. The subjects are non-religious because it was upon these seats that the monks parked their behinds during some of the longer prayer sessions.

Other points of interest in Vendôme include the beautiful 15th-century stone clock tower on **Place St Martin**, the main square; and the château, which is a ruin but is worth climbing up to via a steep path up the hill which dominates the town. From the terraced gardens at the top there are great views. There's a **Tourist Office** on Rue Poterie; tel: 54 77 05 07.

Just outside Vendôme on the D5 is the village of **Villiers-sur-Loir**. Paint is peeling off the outside of the scruffy St Hilaire church, but some bizarre frescoes inside are worth looking out for. The haunted expressions of the faces of tortured bodies are reminiscent of Tibetan Tantric art, but a wall-mounted crib-sheet reveals that the three hideous bodies were painted to represent the toppling pillars of society during the French Revolution. The subversive murals were whitewashed over, until their rediscovery in 1925.

☆ # VOUVRAY WINE-TASTING

Wine-tasting is the reason for visiting this small town on the north bank of the Loire, 10 kilometres east of Tours. From whichever direction you arrive, vineyards will be your introduction. On the N152 from Tours, or from Amboise on the eastern side, terraces of vines in neat rows climb gently up to the north. The D47 south from the A10 motorway undulates over some rolling hills of vines in long, neat sweeps like carefully combed hair, dotted with fine *Domaines* such as Château Goudrelle where a tasting awaits. A more peaceful meandering vineyard route is along the D1 following the valley of the Cisse tributary from Pocé-sur-Cisse north of Amboise.

There are dozens of *caves* in Vouvray itself and in the nearby village of Rochecorbon a few kilometres along the N152 westwards, all offering tours and tastings. However, the best introduction to Vouvray's wines is a visit to the **Maison de Vouvray** in the centre of Rochecorbon where information on all the diverse styles of Vouvray is presented, with tastings designed to illustrate the best of each style.

Sparkling Vouvray is probably the best known. Made almost exclusively from the Chenin Blanc grape, it can be light and bone dry, or rich and sweet; most of the wine, however, is *demi-sec* - somewhere in between. The flowery bouquet and distinctive peachy flavour of a good one can be delicious chilled on a summer's afternoon. Others, sadly, are over-sulphured and can be nasty.

Much more complex are some of the still wines – particularly the sweet ones made in years when 'noble rot' has caused the grapes to shrivel as they do in Sauternes and other great sweet wine producing regions. After ageing for ten years or longer, these Vouvray dessert wines turn a deep golden colour and can be dreamily honeyed and luscious with tangy acidity biting through the sweetness.

Maison de Vouvray, 53, rue du Dr Lebled, Rochecorbon. Tel: 47 52 83 07
Opening times: daily 10am-6pm
Admission: free

Just across the river from Vouvray is Montlouis, which has its own *appellation contrôlée* and several *caves* open to the public. Though lesser known, these wines are of a similar style to Vouvray and are often much better value for money.

WHERE TO STAY

Le Lude
🏠 ✕ 🛏 £

Hôtel Maine, 24, *avenue Saumur,
F-72800 Le Lude
Tel: 43 94 60 54
Open all year*
An exceptionally friendly little family-run hotel near the Château, offering comfortable if somewhat small rooms and excellent value for money. Only four of the 20 rooms have en suite bathrooms, although most of the rest have showers. If you're staying here, you are expected to eat in as well. This is no hardship for anyone with a healthy appetite. The hearty set menu includes delicious soups, wholesome stews and fresh vegetables. The owners will tell you what time to sit down, if you want to finish in time for the *son et lumière* show. But if you're not going, don't go to bed early either or you'll be kept awake by the fireworks. Last orders: lunch 1.30pm; dinner 8.30pm.

Rochecorbon
🏠 ✕ 🛏 £££

Les Hautes Roches, 86, *quai de la Loire, Rochecorbon, F-37210 Vouvray
Tel: 47 52 88 88
H closed mid-Jan - mid-Mar. R closed
Sun eve and Mon Nov-Apr*
If anyone needed reassurance that troglodytic caves in the Loire's tufa-stone quarries can make luxurious accommodation - then here's the proof. The front of the hotel is rather fine and rooms have sweeping vistas up and down the Loire, but the rooms at the back have been hacked out of the rock. All are large and plush with

marble bathrooms. The dining room leads onto a terrace, with great views. There is plenty of river fish on the menu, and an extensive selection of different styles of Vouvray on the wine list. Last orders: lunch 1.30pm; dinner 9.30pm.

Tours
🏠 ✕ 🛏 ££

Hôtel Akilène, 22, *rue du Grand Marché, or 17, rue le la Rôtisserie, F-37000 Tours
Tel: 47 61 46 04
Closed Sun and Mon*
If you're in Tours to enjoy the atmosphere in the Place Plumereau, then the Akilène is the place to stay. The Grand Marché entrance is just a few yards from the square; the decor and general atmosphere are a touch Bohemian and very cosmopolitan with the reception staff claiming to speak five languages between them. The hotel is a wonderful old tall town house with entrances on two streets, restored along with numerous others in the St. Martin district, in traditional style. The rooms are characterful and comfortable, with those on the Rue de la Rôtisserie side considerably quieter. It is a highly popular place, so advance booking is essential. Fairly good value, although the restaurant is a bit pricey. Last orders: lunch 1.30pm; dinner 9.30pm.

Tours

⌂ ✕ ▭ £££

Hôtel Jean Bardet, *Parc de Belmond,*
57, rue Groison, F-37000 Tours
Tel: 47 41 41 11
Closed Feb 21-Mar 8; R closed Mon eve
A luxurious mansion surrounded by
parkland, of a style and atmosphere
usually associated with the most
exclusive country house hotels (the
centre of Tours is just 15 minutes
away). There are 21 large rooms, all
lavishly furnished and individually
decorated. Some have their own balconies with stone balustrades. Eating
in the elegant restaurant is a serious
business with mainly traditional
dishes exquisitely prepared and presented. There is a large conservatory
and a heated swimming pool. It's all
very expensive, but a rare treat. Last
orders: lunch 1.30pm; dinner 9.30pm.

Troo

⌂ ✕ ££

Château de la Voûte, *Troo, F-41800*
Montoire-sur-Loire
Tel: 54 72 52 52
Open all year
A beautiful 16th-century house overlooking the Loir, turned into a
Chambres d'Hôte by the antique-dealer
owner who lives on the ground floor.
Beautiful furniture and *objets d'art*
adorn the spacious, stylish bedrooms
(although one suspects that they may
be carted off to the auction room at
any minute). Huge baths and basins
are all in the same old-world style.
You can have breakfast in your room
or on a terrace with a river view.

Vendôme

⌂ ✕ ✕ ££

Le Vendôme, *15, faubourg Chartrain,*
F-41100 Vendôme
Tel: 54 77 02 88
Closed Jan and Feb
Behind an unprepossessing exterior
near the middle of town is this
pleasant hotel with friendly staff and
comfortable, recently refurbished
bedrooms. The Chapeau Rouge
restaurant within the hotel has more
character; it has a rustic feel to it and
serves generous helpings of a usually
meat-based *Plat du Jour,* and bottles
of quaffable house wine at reasonable
prices - something which is becoming
all too rare in France. There is quite
an extensive *à la carte* menu as well,
but the excellent value of the more
homely fare doesn't come with it.
Last orders: lunch 1.30pm; dinner
8.30pm.

Vernou-sur-Brennes

⌂ ✕ ▭ ££

Hostellerie Perce-Neige, *13, rue
Anatole France, F-37210 Vouvray*
Tel: 47 52 10 04
*H closed Jan. R closed Sun eve and
Mon except June-Sept*
Vernou is a sleepy little rural village a
few kilometres along the D46 from
Vouvray. It is fun to visit on a
Thursday, market day, when it sud-
denly wakes up. The Perce-Neige is a
rather lovely old house and garden,
turned into a cosy, unpretentious
hotel run by a charming couple who
seem to have got discreet attentive-
ness down to a fine art. The rooms
are tastefully understated, though the
food is rather more extravagant and
perhaps not quite as good value as
the accommodation. Last orders:
lunch 2pm; dinner 9pm.

WHERE TO EAT

Montlouis-sur-Loire
✗ ▬ £££

Roc en Val, *4, quai de la Loire, Montlouis-sur-Loire*
Tel: 47 50 81 96
Closed Jan 2-17, Sun eve, Mon lunch, and from Oct-Mar Mon eve

Opposite Vouvray, on the south bank of the Loire, this is a grand, 18th-century mansion in extensive wooded grounds, recently converted into a stylish restaurant serving traditional dishes embellished by modern presentation. The river fish is excellent, and the restaurant is particularly famed for its pastry. The D751 runs between the restaurant and the river, but the dining room is raised, with most tables having views over the water. There is also a terrace where you can eat out in summer. Last orders: lunch 2pm; dinner 9.30pm.

Rochecorbon
✗ ▬ ££

L'Oubliette, *34, rue des Clouets, Rochecorbon,Vouvray*
Tel: 47 52 50 49
Closed last 2 wks Aug; Sun eve and Mon

A troglodyte cave on the D152 between Tours and Vouvray, turned into an intimate, atmospheric restaurant, a perfect place for a romantic dinner. From the front it looks like an ordinary house, but once inside you realise that you're either in a tardis, or in a cave piercing into the white stone cliff. The food is basically traditional with a few *nouvelle cuisine*-ish flourishes to it. Puddings are good and there are some deliciously rich old Vouvray sweet wines to go with

them. Last orders: lunch 1.30pm; dinner 9.30pm.

Tours
✗ ▣ £

Restaurant L' Ecuelle, *5, rue du Grand Marché, Tours*
Tel: 47 66 49 10
Open all year

If you're looking for a budget meal in Tours' old town, you can't do much better than L'Ecuelle. Just a minute's walk from the Place Plumereau, it offers a simple but hearty three-course meal for little more than a beer and sandwich on the square itself. The home-made soup and plates piled high with stew are more the sort of fare you'd expect in one of those excellent French truck-drivers' cafés than this trendy, rebuilt city centre. The decor, however, is more along the lines of a bijou bistro. Last orders: lunch 2pm; dinner 9.30pm.

Tours
✗ ▬ £££

La Roche le Roy, *55, route St Avertin, Tours*
Tel: 47 27 22 00
Closed last 3 wks Aug; Sat lunch and Sun

Some say that La Roche le Roy serves the best food in Tours. Though fairly pricey if you go *à la carte* and choose complementary wines, it is far from the most expensive. Out in the suburb of St Avertin on the south bank of the Cher, this beautiful old 16th-century house can be a tricky place to find. But it's worth seeking out. The presentation of the food is perhaps a bit over the top, but this can be put down to the enthusiasm which pervades the place. In summer, you can eat out in the large, shady garden. Last orders: lunch 1.30pm; dinner 9.30pm.

Vendôme
✕ ▭ ££

Restaurant Daumier, *17, place République, Vendôme*
Tel: 54 77 70 15
Closed Jan, Sun eve and Mon
A lively and characterful little restaurant on the main square, just yards from La Trinité abbey. Exceptionally affable and efficient staff. There's plenty of fish on the menu including *anguilles* (eels), and *rouget* (red mullet). The Touraine house white wine is excellent, and there's a good selection of local cheeses. Last orders: lunch 1.45pm, dinner 9.30pm.

THE CHER AND
THE HEART OF
CHATEAU
COUNTRY

The Cher is a calm, sedate tributary of the Loire, punctuated by some attractive and historic little towns such as Montrichard and St Aignan where you can absorb some of the Loire valley's heritage amid the bustle of market trading as real life goes on around you; the same goes for Loches further south. In all these places the atmosphere is rather more authentic than at some of the major châteaux and great 'sights', allowing you to get close to real rural and market-town France.

The same cannot be said about Chenonceau – one of the most visited of all the châteaux in the Loire valley, but its incontestable beauty should not be missed on any account. Amboise is the other major historic town in this area and this too is a must, even though it teems with tourists in high season.

Away from history, there are plenty of opportunities for walking and swimming along the Cher, as well as wine-tasting and, especially if you have children, a visit to the excellent Beauval Zoo.

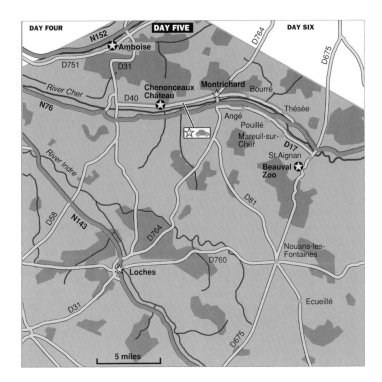

✪ AMBOISE

While Henry VIII was cavorting with his wives and playing tennis at Hampton Court, France was ruled from Amboise by François I in one of the most brilliantly spectacular courts in the Loire valley's glorious royal history. For over a century, beginning in 1440 when Charles VII seized the Château from the Duke of Amboise and made it a royal residence, it was both the nerve centre and the cultural showpiece of the French crown. Mediaeval Amboise was dazzlingly transformed by the splendours of the Renaissance; Leonardo da Vinci spent his final years there advising on the city's art and architecture as well as singing for his supper by pandering to the more childish whims of François I, such as staging firework displays and unbelievably elaborate masked balls for the royal court.

In 1560 came a revolting episode which marked the beginning of the end for Amboise. A Protestant uprising against François II and his Queen (Mary Queen of Scots) failed, and a slaughter of the rebels followed. Hundreds of butchered corpses were hung from the front of the Château and from trees and poles erected round the town. The stench of rotting flesh soon drove the royal party away. Never again was it to be a royal residence, and both Château and city sank into relative obscurity.

Amboise today is a small town, not extending far beyond its historic old quarter which is now saturated with cafés and souvenir boutiques as it throngs with tourists from early spring until autumn. It shows its best face from across the other side of the Loire with the brilliant white Château, towering trees and fine old mansions spectacularly silhouetted against the sky. The **Tourist Office** is on Quai Général de Gaulle; tel: 47 57 09 98.

Fishing on the Loire near Amboise   *Café in the old quarter of Amboise*

Flags and heraldic standards fluttering from the poles which line the steep stone walkway up to the **Château d'Amboise** do no more than hint at the extravagance which was once to be seen in

Amboise. Nor is the extent of the Château more than about a quarter of what it was 500 years ago. As a defunct castle whose day had come and gone, the entire outer fortifications and most of the Renaissance-inspired buildings within were destroyed over the years and it wasn't until the end of the last century that any attempt was made to restore them.

Nevertheless, the parts which remain have been sturdily reconstructed, and the tour is polished and theatrically evocative of the Royal era. Bright-eyed young guides recall the sumptuous banquets and stupendous processions as the court party came and went. They point out with relish interesting snippets such as the low doorway where Charles VIII accidentally killed himself by cracking his head on the beam and suffering fatal concussion. There are also more turgid monologues on details of the architecture, furnishings and tapestries which might be better left to leaflets. The tour, in French only, is not obligatory.

If you choose to explore the Château alone, don't miss the flamboyant Gothic St Hubert's chapel, which once stood on the now obliterated outer ramparts. The other main attractions are in the *Logis du Roi* (King's Apartment) with its contrasting Gothic and Renaissance wings, a clear demonstration of how revolutionary the new Italian-inspired artistic ideas were.

Amboise and its Château

From the Château terrace there are panoramic views over the Loire and the countryside beyond. You can also walk around the gardens which flourish over the foundations of destroyed parts of the Château. A bust of Leonardo da Vinci stands on the site of what was once Amboise's collegiate church. Some say this marks his grave; others that the true whereabouts of his remains will never be known.

Château d'Amboise. Tel: 47 57 00 98
Opening times: Mar-June and Sept-Nov, 9–noon and 2-6.30pm; Jul and Aug, 9am-6.30pm
Admission: adult 30F; child 10F

The aim of Amboise's **Son et Lumière** show is to be as over-the-top as were the extravagant festivities of François I. Entitled *A La Cour du Roi François*, spectacular it certainly is, although not as polished as the shows at Azay-le-Rideau or Le Lude. The cast of between 400 and 500 knights, noblemen, fine ladies, minstrels, jesters and peasants are all drawn from the Amboise population, whose dramatic talent is mixed. It is in French only, but you don't have to understand a lot to follow what is going on.

It fully succeeds in being over the top. There is a lot of bright colour, countless volleys of fireworks and rather too much Leonardo; considering the real genius of the man, it seems a touch undignified to associate him so closely with this royal light entertainment.

The show is performed in the grounds of the Château every Friday and Saturday night from June until the beginning of September, and on various other advertised days. To book, telephone 47 57 14 47
Admission: adult 65F, child 45F

Sadly, there is not a single piece of original work in Amboise by Leonardo da Vinci, the genius scientist, engineer and artist who lived in the city for four years until his death in 1519. However, his rather grand Renaissance house, **Clos Lucé**, has been turned into a museum where you can admire his bedroom, with its four-poster bed, the salon and kitchen. But infinitely more inspiring are the models of his extraordinary and prophetic mechanical inventions. These have been constructed by IBM, the computer company, from his original drawings. Every last detail has been scrupulously adhered to, it is claimed, and only materials available in the 16th century have been used in building the models.

Each exhibit you come to is as mind-blowing as the last, especially when you consider that this was the 16th century: a clockwork self-propelled vehicle, a tank, a helicopter, a fixed-wing aircraft, a parachute, a submarine (based on a very similar principle to that still used today), a swing bridge, a gear box. He understood the potential of steam power, too, as his steam-cannon demonstrates. The impact these machines would have made, had he been able to construct them, we can only guess at. Quite likely they would have been dismissed as the work of the devil. What this exhibition really proves to the layman, in a way that his drawings with all their figures scrawled all over them can't, is that Leonardo da Vinci was a man with ideas and visions which it took Europe at least another 300 years to catch up with.

So why was he messing about designing masked balls for François I?

Château du Clos-Lucé, 2, rue du Clos-Lucé. Tel: 47 57 62 88
Opening times: all year except Jan, 9am-7pm Mar 23-Nov 12; 9am-6pm at other times.

There is a crêperie/snack bar in the garden behind the house
Admission: adult 21F; child 16F

A couple of kilometres out of Amboise on the D31 leading south towards the Cher and Chenonceaux, there is an avenue on the right leading to the famous **Pagode de Chanteloup**. This 38-metre eastern style folly standing in the middle of the Domaine de Chanteloup forest was built in the 1770s on the orders of the Duke of Choiseuil, who wanted a larger version of the pagoda which had been erected a few years previously at Kew Gardens in London. You can climb up for wonderful views over the forest, Amboise and the Loire. Admission 6F; closed on Monday.

☆ BEAUVAL ZOO

Like the superb *Parc Zoologique* at Doué, this is more than a zoo as we understand the concept in Britain. Watching animals as caged exhibits simply isn't the approach. The starting point at Beauval is the animals' habitats: fascinating explanations are given (in French only) of how various animals adapted to the

African savannah, the Amazon rainforest and so on. Mini versions of these habitats have been created as well as is possible in a 25-acre park, with great care taken to allow visitors to observe the animals from discreet viewing points. Apart from keeping the big cats and bears at a safe distance from the public there is very little caging.

Birds are the speciality. In fact, until it was recently extended, Beauval was exclusively an ornithological park which had been established to breed and preserve rare birds from all over the world. Over 300 different species are represented in giant vegetation-filled aviaries and marshy expanses.

Beauval is also a *parc floral* which includes flora indigenous to the animals' and birds' native habitats. Botanists will find thousands of rare plants and flowers amid the lush undergrowth which lines the paths. The Trainestreuilles tributary of the Cher, which flows through the park and is channelled into streams and ponds, makes it possible for these habitats, especially the wetlands, to be created fairly authentically.

What distinguishes a zoo like this from most British ones and makes a visit so worthwhile is the emphasis on education and conservation, rather than simply entertainment. As at Doué, there is a mini zoo for small children, with foals, calves and breeds of tiny goats and donkeys which youngsters can play with and even feed with popcorn or bottles of milk.

Zoo Parc de Beauval, St Aignan-sur-Cher. Tel: 54 75 05 56
Opening times: daily 9am-dusk
Admission: adult 45F, child 20F

✪ CHENONCEAU CHATEAU

'The Queen of the Loire Châteaux' is Chenonceau's unofficial title. For many people, it is simply the most beautiful of them all. Elegant white stone arches span the slow, lazy Cher; sweeping lawns and gardens carpet the banks. Perhaps only Azay-le-Rideau matches Chenonceau's graceful, understated symmetry: a turreted mansion actually *on* the water rather than by it, creating an effect of extraordinary, but restrained elegance, built not for any defensive purpose, but for its own sake.

Probably only Chambord gets as many visitors. The car park outside is immense, with rows of coaches disgorging their daily cargoes during the summer months. But they are all absorbed without the place feeling too claustrophobic – mainly because there are so many different things to do.

Pathways lead through acres of woodland and gardens which are carefully tended but not over-regimented. Dotted around are strange, rather intriguing sculptures of animals – some of them fantastical, such as a bizarre half-rabbit, half-bird creature. You can walk for quite long distances in either direction along the Cher, or hire a rowing boat and go for a spin, four people at a time, out of the moat and on to the river. Other attractions include several cafés and restaurants (including an excellent one in the converted Orangery), and a waxwork museum recreating events from Chenonceau's history; the final scene is of the First World War, when the Château was requisitioned as a hospital.

The tour of the Château itself is one of the best. Instead of a compulsory guided tour, here you can wander from room to room on your own and learn the history of this amazing home at your leisure. Leaflets, in English, are clear and to-the-point. If you do want the full set-menu guided tour you can have it as part of a small group, since most visitors take the DIY option. Tours in English are available.

Château de Chenonceau

Despite being one of the most renowned châteaux of the Loire, Chenonceau has played very little part in the recorded history of France. What emerges as you learn the story of the Château, wandering through the great salons and boudoirs adorned with splendid ceilings and fireplaces, is how it has always been a predominantly female preserve. The original rectangular house was built by Catherine Briconnet; it was confiscated by Henri II and given to his powerful mistress, Diane de Poitiers, who built the exquisite gardens within the moat. Later Henri's wife Catherine de Medici reclaimed it and added the five-arched wing spanning the river.

The Château's *son et lumière* show dramatises the feminine influences and intrigues in *Au temps des Dames de Chenonceau* every Friday evening from mid-June to mid-September. For reservations tel: 47 23 90 07. Admission: 25F.

Château de Chenonceau, Chenonceaux. Tel: 47 23 90 07
Opening times: daily, mid-Feb - mid-Nov 9am-7pm, rest of year 9am-4.30pm
Admission: adult 35F, child 25F

A few kilometres upstream from Chenonceaux on the D40, you come to a fruit distillery called the **Fraise d'Or.** There are free tours and tastings of raspberry, blackberry and strawberry liqueurs among the dozens of different fruits distilled there. Open from 9-11.30am and 2-6pm from March to September.

  ## CHER VALLEY DRIVE

It is not until well upstream of Tours that the Cher begins to reveal its true character. The river, which finds itself lost in the middle of a big city before joining the Loire, is in fact one of the most gentle and graceful of all the tributaries. People who first meet the Cher at Chenonceaux understand this; the waters calmly lapping at the Château's stone foundations seem to mirror its feminine elegance and beautiful proportions.

There is a wonderful variety of things to see and do along the bank-hugging D40 upriver from Chenonceaux, which a signpost announces as the *Route Touristique Coteaux de Cher*. Here are a few of them.

Boat on the graceful River Cher

About 2km out of Chenonceaux, a paved track leads down to the water's edge where *La Bellandre* has her mooring. She is a long, glass-topped **restaurant boat** aboard which you can glide, almost silently, up and down the Cher watching the green bank or twinkling lights float past while you enjoy a meal. There are lunch, dinner and afternoon departures, with tea and *pâtisseries* served on the latter. Each cruise takes about two hours. The route is usually up to Montrichard, where the boat turns round in a difficult manoeuvre, and back again.

Just beyond Montrichard, still on the north bank, is an open stretch of grassy riverbank, a perfect place to stretch your legs. Cross the narrow-gauge railway line just next to the road and head down to the water's edge, then follow a straight, flat path up to the village of Bourré where the Cher tumbles over a rushing weir. You can strip off and have a dip more or less anywhere along this path.

Back on the road, a huge sign invites you to *Visitez les Caves Monmousseau*. To take up this invitation to a wine-tasting, turn left for the cool, cavernous cellars for a free tour taking you through the wine-making processes from grape to bottle, and ending with a tasting. Admittedly, this sparkling wine is neither as good nor as varied as those you may have tasted in Saumur. However, the tour, with English-speaking guides, is interesting and can be regarded as a prelude to some more serious tasting of Touraine wines later in the day, on the other side of the river!

The next place worth a quick stop is **Thésée**, a village dominated by its brilliant white, turreted tufa-stone town hall, which also houses a small museum of locally excavated Roman statues and artefacts together with explanations of the impact of Rome on the Loire Valley. Then head on towards St Aignan, past white cliffs pitted with troglodyte homes and cellars.

St Aignan, a charming place on a château-crowned hill, is worth exploring. As you approach, turn right onto an island linked to the town by two bridges; here you will find an open-air public swimming pool, a very helpful **Tourist Office** (tel: 54 75 22 85) with information on the region, and a car park. The Château is not open to the public and there are few 'sights', but it's a wonderfully atmospheric place to wander round with narrow alleys, steep paved staircases and little courtyards. This is a quintessentially French small town, a lovely place to relax on a café terrace and simply watch the world go by.

If, instead of turning right into St Aignan as you approach from Montrichard, you continue along the road towards Selles-sur-Cher for about two kilometres, there is an interesting little **chapel** on the left worth a quick stop. It stands alone, outside the town, because it was once part of a leper colony.

The D17 along the south bank of the Cher is a narrow, lesser-used route through vineyards sloping up from the river. It is dotted with farming villages where you can stop for *dégustations* of the local earthy *Vin de Touraine*. Try the Clos Roches Blanche in Mareuil-sur-Cher, or Jacques Delaunay's wine in Pouillé further along. There are several more opportunities to taste in Angé, shortly before you arrive back in Montrichard.

☆ LOCHES

High on a hilltop, dominating the small town of Loches, is one of the most extensive and impressive walled cities in the Loire. Yet it still attracts relatively few tourists and unassumingly goes about its business as a small, provincial town which has built up a reputation for growing fine mushrooms and making excellent pastries. An abundance of both is on display in the street market every Saturday. The **Tourist Office** is on Place Marne, near the town centre; tel: 47 59 07 98.

Only once you have climbed the steep stone stairs up to the sturdy, forbidding *Porte Royale* gates of the walled Citadel, enclosing the royal apartments, do you realise the scale of this mighty fortress. The vast crenellated perimeter ramparts, much of them original 10th-century work, are in excellent condition. A *must*, so long as you've got time and energy on your side, is to walk all the way round the top. It is over a kilometre in total and once you have started there is no way down until you have completed the circuit. From this high vantage point, the views over the valleys of the upper Indre and Indrois are unequalled and explain why the hill was of such strategic importance.

A farm near Loches

The official guided tour of the **Château de Loches** uses works of art, documents and other accoutrements as prompts for recounting the history of Loches, which makes for an interesting tour (French only, with English leaflets). The personality who dominates the Château's history, Agnès Sorel, is introduced in the tower of the same name. She was Charles VII's favourite mistress who wielded great power over him and was, according to some, finally poisoned by the Dauphin, the future King Louis XI. (Others believe her premature death at 28 was from natural causes). There are portraits of her looking coquettish with one breast exposed; but her tomb in the Charles VIII room is topped with a reclining, angelic-looking stone effigy.

The *Donjon* is reached along some narrow, cobbled and flagstoned alleys, all within the walled citadel which was once one of the most impenetrable in the Loire. The keep itself was built by Foulques Nerra, and is characteristically forbidding and evocative of the horrific side of feudal Europe, with dungeons and instruments of torture including iron frames in which prisoners were inserted, suspended on chains and left to rot.

Château de Loches, Loches. Tel: 47 59 01 32
Opening times: daily except Wednes 9am–noon and 2–4pm Feb-May and Sept-Nov;
daily 9am–5pm June-Aug
Admission: adult 23F; child 15F

There are two small museums in the citadel, both worth a quick look. One is the **Musée du Terroir** - an exhibition of local crafts - housed in one of the battlement towers. The other is the **Musée Lansyer** - a collection of landscape paintings of the area by the 19th-century local artist of the same name.

Musées Lansyer et Le Terroir. Tel: 47 59 05 45
Opening times: daily except Fri, 9–11.45am and 2–5pm Feb-Nov
Admission: 10F

 A spooky 1½ hour **Nocturnal Tour** of the cleverly floodlit mediaeval Citadel, including the Château and keep, leaves from the Tourist Office on Place Marne. Expect to be regaled with stories of the ghosts which haunt the dungeons and flit over the battlements. There are sometimes tours in English.

Tours leave every evening from July to mid-September at 9pm. Tel: 47 59 07 98 for
information. Cost 25F

If you're driving out of Loches on the D760 towards Montresor, you pass a sign on the left to the *Plan d'Eau*. This is an artificial lake where there is a campsite, excellent swimming, windsurfing, boating, fishing, and a couple of simple restaurants. It's well worth a visit on a hot day.

MONTRICHARD

Richard the Lionheart was once imprisoned in the keep of Montrichard's fortress, whose jagged ruins can be seen pointing skywards as you approach the riverside town on the D40, following the north bank of the Cher. Montrichard is an atmospheric and enjoyable place to wander around especially on Monday, when the town holds a busy agricultural market with farmers bringing in their produce from the surrounding Berry countryside.

If you're looking for a snack lunch in Montrichard, there's an excellent little place called **Le Bistro de la Tour** with tables outside, at the edge of the market place on Rue du Pont.

Climb a narrow stone staircase to the top of the keep for stupendous views over the town, the Cher and, on a clear day, as far as Chenonceaux and Amboise in the distance. The mediaeval houses, clustered around the foot of the castle, some of them with quaint, stone-carved façades, are worth looking out for; so is the very tall Gothic Nanteuil Church with its superb vaulting, on the eastern edge of the town.

A sturdy, Gothic stone bridge crosses the Cher to one of the best beaches on any of the Loire's tributaries. Not only is there excellent swimming with a sandy beach shelving gently into a deep part of the river with picturesque Montrichard beyond, there is also a *Parc de Loisir* with table tennis, a children's playground, and pedalos and canoes for hire. It's great for children, but if you want to get away from the playground atmosphere, there is also a grassy bank without such easy access to the water, where you can sunbathe in relative peace.

WHERE TO STAY

Amboise

⌂ ✕ ▭ £££

Le Choiseuil, *36, quai Charles Guinot, F-37400 Amboise*
Tel: 47 30 45 45
Closed mid-Nov - mid-Mar
This is the smartest place to stay in Amboise. It is a grand, white, 18th-century house set in lush gardens below the Château walls, with panoramic views over the Loire. No detail is overlooked in the large, elegant bedrooms with marble bathrooms. The service is friendly and efficient and the restaurant is excellent, serving some of the best prepared and most exquisitely presented food in the region, with plenty of fish and game. Not a place to miss, if it's within your price bracket. Last orders: lunch 2pm; dinner 9.15pm.

Amboise

⌂ ✕ ▭ £

Hôtel du Lion d'Or, *17, quai Charles Guinot, F-37400 Amboise*
Tel: 47 57 00 23
Closed Jan - mid-Feb; R closed Sun and Mon eve Nov-Mar
A comfortable little hotel nestling at the foot of the Château's formidable ramparts, in the old town. It's a friendly place with small but attractively decorated rooms and a restaurant serving traditional food. The home-baked bread is delicious. Last orders: lunch: 2pm; dinner 9pm.

Chargé

⌂ ✕ ▭ ££

Château de Pray, *Chargé, F-37400 Amboise*
Tel: 47 57 23 67
Closed Jan 1-Feb 15
A beautiful château, parts of which are 700 years old, on a cliff high above the Loire a few kilometres upstream from Amboise on the road to Chaumont. An aura of grandeur is balanced by the homely atmosphere created by friendly staff. The bedrooms, all with full bathrooms, are spacious and comfortable; the dining room is attractive with windowside tables enjoying stunning views. In summer, *apéritifs* are served on a garden terrace. You can stay here only on a half-board basis. Last orders: lunch 2pm; dinner 9pm.

Loches

⌂ ✕ ▭ ££

Hôtel George Sand, *39, rue Quintefol, F-37600 Loches*
Tel: 47 59 39 74
Closed Nov 27-Dec 27
A 17th-century post house on the historic town's main street, overshadowed by the vast Château. The back is adorned with hanging baskets and overlooks the lapping waters of the Indre. There are some wonderful old beams, stone fireplaces and a spiral staircase leading up to the bedrooms, all of which are comfortable and individually furnished and decorated; those with a river view are delightful. There's a waterside terrace for drinks, and several of the elegant restaurant's tables overlook the water as customers enjoy traditional fare

made from fresh ingredients. Last
orders: lunch 2pm; dinner 9.30pm.

Thésée
🏠 ✕ 🚍 £

La Mansio, *9, rue Nationale,
F-41140 Thésée-la-Romain
Tel: 54 71 40 07
Closed Jan; R closed Tues eve and
Wednes, Oct-Mar*
A quaint little *Logis de France* in the
village famous for its Roman ruins.
There is a small garden at the back

and the Cher is just a short walk
away. A bridge crosses over to the
village of Pouillé on the south bank
where there are several *caves* where
you can taste Touraine wines. A variety of these are served with large portions of traditional wholesome fare in
the restaurant. The rooms are basic,
but comfortable; some have en suite
showers and a couple have baths. If
you're staying there, you are expected to eat in the restaurant. Last
orders: lunch 2pm; dinner 9.30pm.

WHERE TO EAT

Amboise
✕ 🚍 ££

Les Bateliers, *L'Entrepont, 7, rue
Commire, Amboise
Tel: 47 30 49 49
Closed Sun eve Nov-Feb*
A beautifully situated restaurant on
an island in the Loire with broad
views of the river, town and Château
which at night is romantically floodlit. The food is traditional and well-
prepared, if unexciting. There is also
a waterside terrace where you can
have a drink in summer, or enjoy a
game of boules. Last orders: lunch
2.30pm; dinner 10pm.

Chenonceaux
✕ 🚍 ££

L'Orangerie, *Château de
Chenonceau, Chenonceaux
Tel: 47 23 91 97
Open Mar 1-Nov 11 for lunch only*
It's rare to find a quality restaurant
cheek by jowl with a major tourist
attraction. Yet the converted
orangery in the grounds of the
Château is nothing less, and quite

reasonably priced at that. It's a large,
airy room with scores of tables, looking out across manicured lawns
towards the Château. The cooking is
traditional French, simply presented
and delicious. In summer, don't even
think of trying to get a table without
booking. Last orders: 3pm.

Montrichard
✕ 🚍 ££

Le Grill du Passeur, *2, rue du Bout
du Pont, Montrichard
Tel: 54 32 06 80
Open all year*
You're unlikely to have either the
best or the cheapest meal of your stay
in the Loire here. It merits a mention
because of its extraordinary location:
the tiny restaurant is actually part of
the old stone bridge, looking like a
fortified turret defending the town
from any assailants who may be pad-
dling up the Cher. Inside it's dark,
rustic, a bit overpriced, and very
friendly. The food is mainly steaks
and grilled fish. Last orders: lunch
2pm; dinner 10pm.

BLOIS AND THE
HUNTING
CHATEAUX

Travelling upstream from Tours and Amboise, you move into the densest part of the Loire Valley's château country. Two of the greatest attractions in the entire region dominate the sight-seeing options, with enough history and architecture to keep most people busy for several days. One of these is Blois, considered by many to be among the most beautiful cities in France. However, it is the overall mien of its exterior, rather than its individual sights, which gives it this distinction, inviting leisurely exploration on foot. A visit to the city's famous chocolate factory is one suggested piece of light relief amid all the culture.

The monstrous Château de Chambord is less universally acclaimed for its beauty, but as the largest and undoubtably the most awesome château of all, it should certainly not be missed. Of the several less famous châteaux in the region, two of particular interest are the 'hunting lodge' of Cheverny and the startling white Loire-side Chaumont.

Ways of exploring the heart of the mysterious Sologne country are suggested in Day Seven, but among the options in this chapter is a visit to the region's principal town, Romorantin, down towards its southern boundary. Here, attractions range from the outstanding *Solognot* country life museum to an exhibition of racing cars.

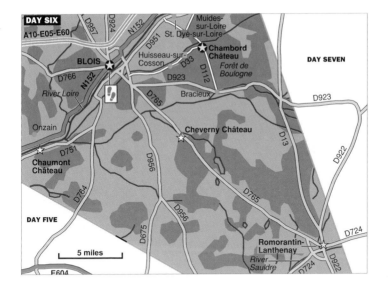

D957 D924 N152
Muides-sur-Loire
St. Dyé-sur-Loire
BLOIS
Huisseau-sur-Cosson
D951 D33
Chambord Château
DAY SEVEN
Forêt de Boulogne
D766 N152
D923 D112
River Loire
D765
Bracieux
D923
Onzain
Cheverny Château
D13
D751
D956
D922
Chaumont Château
D764
D765
DAY FIVE
D956
D675 D956
Romorantin-Lanthenay
D724
5 miles
River Sauldre
D724 D922
E604

BLOIS

Approach Blois over the Pont Jacques Gabriel from the south if you possibly can. It's hard to imagine a city skyline more majestic than these stone towers and steeples rising above an old town of blue-tiled houses packed haphazardly together on a hill falling sharply down to the Loire, with a massive château dominating the whole scene.

Its history, architecture, aura and sheer beauty make the city one of the most famous and most visited in the entire Loire valley. Industry, however, has largely passed it by (the Poulain chocolate factory is a sweet exception), leaving Blois only a fraction of the size of Angers, Tours or Orléans; the result is a dense concentration of monuments, architectural treasures and ancient steets, spanning an expanse of history. If there's one city in the Loire valley really worth spending time in, this is it.

But the magic of Blois is due to more than the various sights and attractions which feature on most tourist itineraries. Certainly, the Château and Cathedral are worth visiting, but it is the beautifully preserved and restored whole which gives the city its singular charm. Blois is not a place for rushing straight to the famous monuments. Instead, get a feel for the city's exterior by

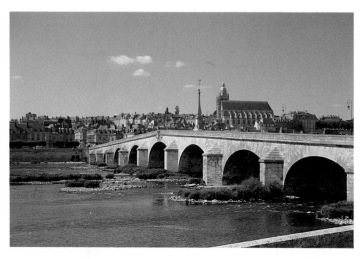

The Pont Jacques Gabriel at Blois

wandering through the streets, squares and gardens on foot; this is easily done although there some knee-straining gradients. If you explore Blois in this way, your later visit to the sights themselves will be hugely enriched.

Parking in Blois is appalling. An excellent alternative to the frustration of full car parks, traffic jams and permanently-occupied meters is to leave your car south of the river and walk across the bridge.

A CITY WALK

Walking across the 18th-century Pont Jacques Gabriel towards Blois is rather like approaching a cinema screen – the nearer you get, the further you have to put your head back to take in the full panorama. To become an extra in the picture, turn left at the Rond-Point de la Résistance at the end of the bridge, and follow the quayside for a few hundred yards down to Rue Trois Marchands. Turn right, passing the lovely old triple-spired 12th- and 13th-century **St Nicholas church**, originally a Benedictine monastery. This unusually successful blend of Romanesque and Gothic is well worth a look; on a summer's day, the thick bulk of its stone wall make it a cool place to escape the heat for a few minutes.

A series of worn stone staircases climb up from the north-east corner of the church to the Place du Château where you'll deserve a drink or a snack lunch in one of the many cafés whose hundreds of tables collectively colonise the great esplanade outside the castle, presided over by an awkward-looking statue of King Louis XII on horseback. From here, the Château shows its most austere, forbidding face while the view to the south and east is of terraced gardens, the jumbled roofs of mediaeval houses, and long sweeps of the Loire and its flood-plain beyond.

Leisurely yet keenly fought games of *boules* are contested between beret-clad men on the beaten earth between the privet hedges and herbaceous borders of the gardens leading down to the heart of the mediaeval quarter. Here you can wander down pedestrianised alleys overhung by tall, timber-framed houses and mansions – some of them built around cool courtyards shyly hiding beyond wrought-iron gates. Thread your way through the maze of streets, taking care not to miss the **Hôtel de la Chancellerie** – a superb, stone-carved mansion and courtyard on Rue St Martin. Another splendid mediaeval house, dating from the royal age when countless noblemen and courtiers lived in Blois, is the **Maison des Acrobates**, on the Rue du Palais between the top of the Denis-Papin staircase and the Place St Louis outside the cathedral: look for the carved acrobats and jugglers on the posts outside the timbered façade.

If you lose your bearings and want to find the way back to the bridge, try following your nose. This will probably bring you onto Rue Denis Papin, the characterful straight road which slices through the mediaeval quarter, lined with one mouthwatering *chocolaterie* after another. If you can resist the overpoweringly enticing aromas of the glistening works of art in the windows, make your abstemious way straight down to the aptly-named Rond-Point de la Résistance, and back across the river.

There is a large and helpful **Tourist Office** (tel: 54 74 06 49) near the Château at 3, avenue Jean Laigret with maps and plenty of information on things to see and do in Blois and the surrounding region.

It is impossible to categorise the **Château de Blois** as belonging to any particular historical style or tradition. Stand in the inner courtyard and you are surrounded by a hotch-potch of every architectural era from the 13th-century *Grande Salle* and *Tour du Foix*, dating from when the Château was a feudal defensive fortress, through glorious Renaissance masterpieces such as the François I wings, to the classically-styled 17th-century Gaston d'Orléans wing. A tour of the Château introduces you to the history of Blois through its architecture and associations, with relatively few objects and ornaments to detain you. Mercifully, you can explore the interior without a guide.

The inner courtyard itself is by far the most interesting part, with its fascinating amalgam of architectural styles. Do not miss the royal apartments in the François I wing. On the first floor is Catherine de Medici's room, where you can see her 237 secret cupboards, hidden behind intricately carved wooden panels and opened by means of pedals hidden in the skirting boards. If you're feeling in a gruesome mood, go upstairs and follow in your printed leaflet the gory details of how King Henri III personally murdered the Duc de Guise after a chase from chamber to chamber, a story worthy of a good thriller.

There are two museums within the walls, each warranting a quick visit. One is the **Archaeological Museum** where there is a useful 15-minute audio-visual presentation, in French, on the Château, together with some Roman remains excavated in Blois. The other is the **Musée des Beaux-Arts** where some 16th- and 17th-century paintings, including a portrait of Marie de Medici by Rubens, are exhibited. Entrance to both is included in the Château's admission charge.

Les Esprits Aiment la Nuit – spirits prefer the night – is the title of the ethereal *son et lumière* show in the Château which embellishes with magic touches stories surrounding Joan of Arc, Catherine de Medici and other women associated with its history. The 45-minute performance, in French, is staged every night from mid-March to mid-September at 10.30pm in French and 11.30pm in English. Tel: 54 74 06 49 for details and bookings. Admission: adult 60F; child 30F.

Château de Blois. Tel: 54 78 06 62
Opening times: daily all year, mid-Mar - mid-Nov 9am-6pm, rest of year 9am-noon and 2-5pm
Admission: adult 38F; child 15F

A freak whirlwind in 1687 is said to have almost completely destoyed the **Cathedral of St Louis**, whose origins date back to the 10th century; it is not known quite how much of this early

Blois

work was still intact then. But most of what stands today was built rapidly, in Gothic style, soon after the destruction. Many visitors are disappointed by the result.

The crypt, however, has a powerful atmosphere which is quite distinct from the rest of the cathedral – especially if you are lucky enough to have it to yourself for a few minutes (try the very early morning). It was built in the 10th century to accommodate pilgrims to the shrine of St Comblée, a local martyr on whose tomb the original church was built. Amid the quiet, something of this ancient aura lives on.

There are no published opening or closing times, although the cathedral is locked at night. If you want to visit the crypt alone, you could try knocking on a side door while the cathedral is closed to see if an obliging priest might let you in

Chocoholics Anonymous, roll up! As you probably gathered while wandering past myriad *chocolatiers* in the old town, Blois is a chocolate capital. The place to learn all about it is at the **Poulain Chocolate Factory**, on Avenue Gambetta near the railway station. The factory is one of Blois' principal industries, employing about 1,000 people, and producing over 30,000 tons of high-quality chocolate a year.

Don't expect to go there and just gorge. There's an hour-long tour before you even have your first nibble. You learn, through a series of exhibitions, about the life and times of Auguste Poulain, a local lad of lowly birth in the early 19th century, who became a confectioner. He had a steam tug built to pull barges of cocoa and sugar up from Nantes, where they had arrived from the New World; he then set himself the goal of making the finest chocolate in France.

Next you visit the factory floor itself, to ogle at the spectacle of mind-bogglingly enormous *marmites* of bubbling brown chocolate, amid the all-pervading smell of sweet, rich indulgence. Anyone whose childhood featured Roald Dahl's *Charlie and the Chocolate Factory* will understand how true to life this work of fiction is.

When they reach the final stage of the tour – the sampling – some visitors find that they have already enhaled enough chocolate, and that a further single square would be likely to make them sick!

Chocolatier Poulain, Rue Gambetta, Blois. Tel: 54 74 39 21
Opening times: Mon-Fri all year; tours at 8.45 & 10am, 1.30 & 2.45pm
Admission: 5F

⭐ CHAMBORD CHATEAU

Turn the corner at the end of the straight D112 which cuts across the *Forêt de Boulogne* from the market town of Bracieux and behold a dazzling sight. If the sun is shining from behind, you might literally have to shield your eyes from the glare reflected off monstrous white Chambord, the greatest of all the châteaux of the Loire valley.

The greatest, that is, in terms of size. It was built on the orders of King François I (he of the pyrotechnics and court extravaganzas in Amboise) ostensibly as a hunting lodge on the edge of the Sologne region, but in reality it is a monument to his boundlessly expanding ego and megalomania. The list of superlative statistics is endless: Chambord is larger even than the Palace of Versailles; it has 440 rooms, 365 windows, a forest of 365 chimneys - one for every day of the year, 15 principal and a staggering 70 further staircases. It is said to have taken the equivalent of 1,800 men working constantly for 12 years to build it and the grounds are enclosed within France's longest wall, 32 kilometres long. Apart from the fact that Chambord was still unfinished at his death in 1547, the King's only unfulfilled ambition for the Château was the diversion of the Loire to fill a suitably majestic moat.

Château de Chambord and its forest of chimneys

Yet for all the grandeur, it is hard to see the Château as any more beautiful than the character of the ostentatious, unfathomably conceited man who inspired it. Its boisterous, loud exterior is in complete contrast to the feminine charm of Azay-le-Rideau or Chenonceau. But on no account miss the awesome spectacle of this mammoth folly rising out of the forest, where the King would come for the occasional spot of hunting, bringing with him an entourage several thousand strong, with all their gear borne on 12,000 horses.

You can wander freely in Chambord's extensive grounds and parkland without paying an entrance fee. Inside, there's a good 15-minute audio-visual introduction, shown in English as well as French, explaining the history of the Château and evocatively bringing to life its royal era. This film is well worth seeing before you begin your hike from cavernous hall to echoing salon, which you can do at your own pace without a guide. There is nothing particularly remarkable to see in terms of furnishings or works of art; the two unmissable points of interest are the famous double spiral staircase on which people can climb or descend while neither meeting nor losing sight of each other, and the roof terrace with expansive views over the *Forêt de Boulogne* from which wives and mistresses used to watch their menfolk out hunting.

The *son et lumière* concept was invented at Chambord in 1952. The Château does have a magnificent setting for this kind of show, staged on the bank of the Cosson tributary with the great forest behind. The performance is called *Le Combat du Jour et de la Nuit* – the conflict between night and day - and dramatises the royal hunting age. Performances are on Friday, Saturday and Sunday from mid-April to the end of May, and every evening from mid-June to the end of September. The shows, in French, last 35 minutes starting between 9.30pm and 10.45pm, depending on the season. For details and bookings tel: 54 20 31 32. Admission: adult 50F; child 35F.

Château de Chambord, Bracieux. Tel: 54 20 31 32
Opening times: all year except public holidays - May, June and Sept 9am-5pm; Jul and Aug 9am-6pm; Oct-Apr 9.30-11.45am and 2-4.45pm
Admission: adult 31F, child 16F

 Twice a day, visitors to the Château are treated to a spectacular display of dressage which evokes the great equestrian era of Louis XV's reign, when a cavalry regiment was based here. The *Spectacle d'Art Equestre* takes place in a walled courtyard in the Château grounds, bedecked with standards and banners. The horses thunder in to the sounds of fanfares and rousing music, ridden by fine-looking young men and women in the elaborate Louis XV garb of flowing coats and ermine-fringed hats.

The show is more theatre with a touch of circus thrown in than pure dressage – with the *pièce de résistance* being the horses leaping over flaming crossbars. No part of the display is particularly refined or polished, but this doesn't stop the children present oohing and aahing with delight.

Spectacle d'Art Equestre, Château de Chambord. Tel: 54 20 31 01
Performances every day from May to September, at 11.45am and 5pm
Admission: adult 40F, child 25F

The stabling for the thousands of horses which lived at Chambord during the hunting and cavalry eras now plays its

The Spectacle d'Art Equestre at Chambord

part in the tourism effort. The **Royal Stables** make up a small village of shops, cafés and bars. This is also the place to go to hire bicycles (25F an hour) to ride round the Château grounds or into the *Forêt de Boulogne*. You can also hire well-groomed horses to ride in the 11,000-acre forest for 95F an hour, but you must be able to demonstrate competent horsemanship; or for 45F a person, you can enjoy a 45-minute trot around the grounds in a horse-drawn carriage.

The *Forêt de Boulogne* south of Chambord, can be an excellent place to stop for a picnic. However, much of the forest is out of bounds as a *Réserve Nationale de Chasse*. If you are driving away from Chambord on the D112 towards Bracieux, leave behind you the signs announcing the *Parc de Chambord*, take one of the narrow lanes off to the right, and find a shaded clearing in the bracken undergrowth.

☆ CHAUMONT CHATEAU

Chaumont is one of the most beautifully situated of all the châteaux in the Loire Valley. Set on a cliff high above the Loire, it is worth visiting for the view from its terrace alone: the sight of the river curving off towards the horizon in both directions creates an awesome sense of space and majesty. The Château itself, when viewed from a distance, is no less beautiful. Its sturdy walls and pepperpot towers rise, brilliantly white, out of some dense hilly forest with the village of Chaumont-sur-Loire and the lovely old stone bridge across to Onzain on the north bank at its feet.

A tour of the Château de Chaumont's interior is harder to enthuse about. Only the most dedicated will want to be escorted through the numerous rooms full of Aubusson tapestries and works of Renaissance art. Many people find that they get a much more authentic feel for Chaumont by wandering through the grounds, shaded by huge cedar trees which lend a balmy scent to the air. They can read (in a leaflet published in English) of the Château's early days as a 15th-century feudal fortress; and how it later became the home of the beautiful Diane of Poitiers, mistress of King Henri II, after she was evicted from Chenonceau following his death.

The extensive and magnificent stables, built in the 19th century by the then owners Prince Amadée de Broglie and his wife Marie, make an interesting tour. There are porcelain troughs, stables lined with velvet, tiny stables for children's ponies, and an enormous one for the elephant donated to Marie by a visiting Indian Maharajah.

Château de Chaumont, Chaumont-sur-Loire. Tel: 54 20 98 03
Opening times: Apr-Sept 9am-6pm; Oct-Mar 9am-4.30pm
Admission to Château, grounds and stables: adult 25F; child 6F

Across the Loire from Chaumont, a few kilometres north is the village of **Onzain** which has a tourist office containing a small wine museum. Here you can taste the characterful but little-known *appellation* Touraine-Mesland. The dry whites made from the Sauvignon grape are a good Sancerre alternative. There are also reds and rosés made from the Beaujolais Gamay grape.

BALLOONING

If you're in the Loire Valley between June and September and feel like trying an exciting way to view the river, châteaux and countryside from a completely difference perspective, why not take a flight in a hot air balloon? No excuses such as age or state of health are acceptable - the Bombard Society which organises flights has taken a 90-year-old lady up in her wheelchair! She loved it.

Flights are in the early morning, and in the evening shortly before dusk; they generally leave from the grounds of a château or large hotel - as near as possible to where the majority of passengers for any particular flight are staying. The experience is a wonderful one as up to eight passengers float off over the tree-tops and vineyards, high above the Loire, over a majestic château, or wherever the wind happens to blow that day. A ground crew follows in a minibus to meet the balloon in whatever field or piece of open land it comes down. As the balloon is packed away, Champagne is produced and shared with locals who invariably arrive on the scene to watch the fun.

The cost is around 1,350F for a flight of about an hour. Cancellations on account of weather are frequent, with money refunded in full. You can book a balloon flight with the Bombard Society in any French travel agent, or by telephoning 80 26 63 30 (English spoken).

Crossing the Loire by balloon near Château de Chaumont

☆ ## CHEVERNY CHATEAU

This is a minor château, on the D765 from Blois to Romorantin, which will appeal to classical purists for its architecture and ornaments and to hunting enthusiasts for its pack of hounds, trophy room and eminence as one of the most exclusive hunts in the Sologne region.

The Château itself is a large and sumptuous 17th-century mansion set in an expansive park (most of which is out of bounds to visitors). The classical façade is as white as a peeled potato, with a black slate roof completing its perfectly symmetrical proportions. It was finished in 1634 for Count Henri Hurault de Cheverny, descendants of whom still own and live in the Château. Over the centuries the family has accumulated fabulous collections of art, furniture and armour which can be viewed in panelled rooms with painted ceilings. As in other smaller châteaux such as Montgeoffroy, it is the atmosphere engendered by the fact that this is a real home and not merely a museum which makes Cheverny worth visiting. Here you can either take a guided tour in French or wander around on your own with leaflets in English.

The **Hunting Museum** turns out to be a collection of over 2,000 pairs of antlers proudly on display, conjuring up images of a bloody massacre. You won't escape the yelping of the 90-strong Cheverny hunting pack in the kennels, especially if you happen to be there at feeding time (usually between 3 and 5pm) when hunks of meat are thrown to the ravenous, frenzied hounds. On certain days between November and Easter – usually twice a week – the hunt meets at Cheverny and sets off for the forests of the Sologne to the shrill reverberation of horns. Times at which the hunt meets are available at the booking office or by telephoning the Château.

A lengthy *son et lumière* performance with hunting as its theme and haunting sound effects is staged at 10pm on the last three Saturdays in July and August. Admission: 36F.

Château de Cheverny, Cour-Cheverny. Tel: 54 79 96 29
Opening times: daily, Apr-Oct 9.15am-6.45pm, May-Sept 9.30am-noon and
2-4.30pm
Admission: adult 28F; child 14F

Château de Cheverny

In the main square of the small market town of **Bracieux** between Cour-Cheverny and Chambord, there is a wonderful old 16th-century wooden-pillared covered market. On Thursday, market day, it becomes the hub of local agricultural activity; on other days you can explore it in peace.

ROMORANTIN-LANTHENAY

Generally referred to simply as Romorantin, this small town has long been the butt of French jokes about remoteness and provincial naïvety. This is probably born out of the reputation the Sologne region has for insularity; and for the small-town feel which still pervades the place today, accounting for its laid back sort of charm.

Nevertheless Romorantin does have a few claims to historical fame, including being the place where François I grew up, and where he later brought Leonardo da Vinci to design a glorious château for his mother, Louise de Savoie. Had not both mother and Leonardo died before the plans came to fruition, perhaps Romorantin would not be the sleepy place it is today. Its next important historical event seems to have been in 1969: the winning of the motor-racing Formula One World Championship by the local car manufacturer Matra.

Locally, Romorantin is often referred to as the capital of the Sologne, although this distinction does not involve any administrative role. There are some fine old Renaissance houses in the centre of town and some vestigial remains of the 15th-century château where François I spent his childhood. However, the fascinating Sologne Museum provides a far better reason for visiting the town.

 The overall effect of a visit to the **Sologne Museum**, housed in the town hall, is to paint a picture blending the realism and the romance of life out in the strange and isolated Sologne. Particularly interesting are the re-constructed peasants' cottage, and the clog-maker's workshop. Together, they build up a powerful image of cottage industry and peasant community life, of a genre rather like that immortalised by Laurie Lee in his writings on England's Cotswold villages. There are also exhibitions on the geology, explaining how beneath the topsoil there is a bed of clay which prevents rainwater from draining away, instead creating the soggy ground and marshland for which the Sologne is known, and equally interesting exhibitions of *Solognot* wildlife, agriculture, costumes and other traditions.

Musée de Sologne, Mairie de Romorantin. Tel: 54 76 07 06
Opening times: all year 10-11.30am and 2-3.30pm; closed Tues and Sun am
Admission: adult 8F; child 4F

 After Matra's great victory in 1969, a **Racing Car Museum** was established near the Matra factory over on the east side of the town. The 1969 winning car is there as well as many others; more cerebrally stimulating are the exhibitions showing the technical development of the racing car and how various scientific advances have come about as side-effects. There is also a motor sports library, with endless technical details, but this really is only for true enthusiasts.

Musée de la Course Automobile, 29, faubourg d'Orléans. Tel: 54 76 07 06
Opening times: all year 10-11.30am and 2-3.30pm; closed Tues and Sun am
Admission: adult 8F; child 4F

At Romorantin, the **River Sauldre** disintegrates into a series of channels and islets before regaining its composure and flowing on to join the Cher. The eight or so bridges which join these islets provide some enchanting views over the river, linking up to make an excellent short walk.

WHERE TO STAY

Blois
🏠 ✕ 🛏 *££*
Le Relais Bleu du Château, *22, rue Porte Côte, F-41000 Blois*
Tel: 54 78 20 24
Open all year
Conveniently situated in the middle of Blois just a couple of minutes' walk from the château entrance, this recently restored old hotel is comfortable, attractive and good value for money. The rooms are tastefully decorated and well equipped; the restaurant, spilling out onto a delightful courtyard where you can eat out in summer, is popular with locals. There are excellent fish and game dishes and an extensive cheese board. Last orders: lunch 1.30pm; dinner 9.30pm.

Cheverny
🏠 ✕ 🛏 *£££*
Château du Breuil, *Route de Fougère-sur-Bievres, F-41700 Cheverny*
Tel: 54 44 20 20
H closed Dec-Feb
R closed Sun eve and Mon
A long, shaded driveway off the D52 a couple of miles out of Cour-Cheverny, leads up to the fine old mansion surrounded by lawns sweeping down to the edge of dense woodland. There are 16 individually

finished bedrooms, furnished with fine antiques. You can have an *apéritif* out on the lawn before going through to the twin dining rooms which are rather sparsely decorated although the traditional food, imaginatively presented, is excellent. You are expected to eat in the restaurant if you are staying there. Last orders: lunch 2pm; dinner 10pm.

Huisseau-sur-Cosson
🏠 ✕ 🛏 *££*
Château de Nanteuil, *Huisseau-sur-Cosson, F-41350 Vineuil*
Tel: 54 42 61 98
H closed Jan and 3rd wk Nov
R closed Mon, and Tues lunch
A large country house just off the D33 within 15 minutes of both Blois and Chambord on the edge of the River Cosson, which is diverted to form Chambord's moat. Bedrooms are pleasant and unpretentious, with some rooms having river views. A condition of staying there is that you must eat in the restaurant; this is certainly no hardship - in summer you can sit out on the waterside terrace and enjoy delicious fish from the Cosson, or game from the Sologne cooked to traditional recipes. Last orders: lunch 2pm; dinner 9.30pm.

Muides-sur-Loire

⌂ ▭ £££

Château de Colliers, *Muides-sur-Loire, F-41500 Mer*
Tel: 54 87 50 75
Closed Nov-Feb

Charming Christian and Marie-France de Gélis, whose family has owned this attractive 17th-century mansion for over 200 years, have turned it into a very classy *Chambres d'Hôte*. Guests are made to feel welcome and at ease as they are shown up to their attractively furnished bedrooms, all of which have views over a small bird sanctuary island in the Loire below. There is no restaurant, but on advance request guests are welcomed to the family dinner table.

Onzain

⌂ ✕ ▭ ££££

Domaine des Hauts de Loire, *F-41150 Onzain*
Tel: 54 20 83 41
Closed Dec-Feb

This is another of those places, like Château d'Artigny on the Indre for example, worthy of serious consideration if you're going to push the boat out just once during your tour of the Loire Valley. It's not that this ivy-clad former hunting lodge is particularly majestic or imposing - rather the reverse: it's a discreet, elegant sort of place, set in a beautiful wooded park, next to a lake. The rooms are charmingly decorated with minute attention to detail; the service makes you feel like an honoured guest and the superlative food must be the best in a very wide area. Only the prices may keep you away. Last orders lunch 2pm; dinner 9pm.

St Dyé-sur-Loire

⌂ ✕ ▭ ££

Manoir Bel Air, *St Dyé-sur-Loire, F-41500 Mer*
Tel: 54 81 60 10
Closed mid-Jan - mid-Feb

St Dyé-sur-Loire is a rather charmless village sprawled along the main D 951. But don't be put off, Manoir Bel Air is a delightful 17th-century house down by the riverside, on a charming lane perfect for pre-prandial strolls. There are some small, but very characterful, bedrooms in the oldest part of the house; and larger, more comfortable ones in the period-style modern extension. Most have river views. In summer, you can eat out on the terrace; the cooking is traditional, using fresh, local ingredients. Last orders: lunch 2.30pm; dinner 9.30pm.

WHERE TO EAT

Blois
✕ ▭ £££

La Péniche, *Promenade du Mail, Blois*
Tel: 54 74 37 23
Closed Sun
This is an old grain barge moored down on the quay, which has been turned into a classy restaurant serving excellent river fish dishes and seafood, some of which can be viewed in seawater tanks on board. The dining area is actually the barge's hold, but windows have been cut out so that you can sit and watch the Loire flowing past. Last orders: lunch 2pm; dinner 9.30pm.

Blois
✕ ▭ £

La Bocca d'Or, *15, rue Haute, Blois*
Tel: 54 78 04 74
Closed Sun, Mon lunch and all Jan and Feb
Inhabitants of Blois seem to agree that La Bocca d'Or has the best food in town, although it certainly isn't cheap. Despite its name, there is nothing Italian about it - the food is traditionally French, well presented and served in generous portions. The chef takes particular pride in his colourful puddings. Last orders: lunch 1.30pm; dinner 9pm.

Bracieux
✕ ▭ £££

Le Relais de Bracieux, *Bracieux*
Tel: 54 46 41 22
Closed Jan; Tues eve and Wednes
Follow the footsteps of the Prince of Wales and many other celebrities to this famous restaurant boasting two Michelin rosettes. The setting, in this peaceful village not more than ten minutes' drive from Cheverny or Chambord, is as attractive as the exquisitely presented modern cooking. Vegetarian dishes are a speciality, although plenty of meat, fish and seafood are also served. Prices are quite reasonable, considering the quality and the acclaim of this restaurant. Booking well in advance is essential. Last orders: lunch 1.30pm; dinner 9pm.

Romorantin-Lanthenay
☙ ▭ ££

Le Colombier, *10, place du Vieux-Marché, Romorantin-Lanthenay*
Tel: 54 76 12 76
Closed Jan 15-Feb 15
This is a place to go if you have really worked up an appetite. The food is regional *Solognot*, rustic and delicious; steaming stews and roast game are served in huge portions. Despite all this wholesome fare, it's a small place with the decor verging on twee. There are also a few bedrooms upstairs, but it is for the food that Le Colombier is recommended. On week-days it is extremely good value for money; at weekends, a little less so. Last orders: lunch 1.15pm; dinner 8.30pm.

ORLEANS, THE SOLOGNE AND THE UPPER LOIRE

Orléans suffered such devastation during the Second World War, that there are few 'sights' left to see. Nevertheless, this major Loire city has a tremendous history behind it, fully exploited through its various museums. Joan of Arc, the 'Maid of Orleans' is the most famous character with a museum all to herself, and also appears in the other main attractions worth seeing – St Croix Cathedral and the Historic Museum.

Few tourists choose to stay in central Orléans; however, in the city's picturesque, villagey suburbs of Olivet and St Hilaire–St Mesmin there are some excellent waterside hotels and restaurants. Nearby is the glorious *Parc Floral de La Source* where you can walk for miles admiring the unbelievable expanses of flowers in bloom.

This far up the Loire, the châteaux become fewer and further between; however, forbidding feudal Meung is worth a visit. From here, the more adventurous might throw caution to the wind and take up the option of floating down to the town of Beaugency in a kayak. The only other château on the day's itinerary is the one at Gien which now houses a hunting museum. Also upstream of Orléans is the wonderfully atmospheric St Benoît monastery; and much further up, the winophile's shrine of Sancerre where the Loire's best wine is produced.

That just leaves the mysterious and magical land of the Sologne south of Orléans, touched on in the last chapter, to be explored in a drive through the heart of the region.

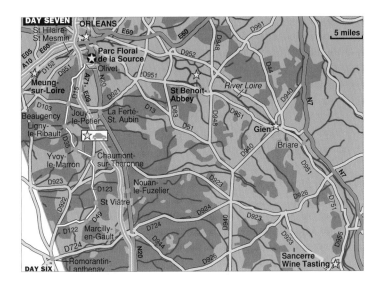

 ☆ **GIEN**

There are several good reasons for stopping to explore this attractive little town on the north bank of the Loire, 60 kilometres upstream of Orléans. It makes an excellent break if you're making the trip to Sancerre; there is an interesting hunting museum and a factory making the town's famous *faïence*, glazed earthenware, both of which make worthwhile visits. The riverside promenade, lined with shops, restaurants and cafés where you can stop and have a drink or snack on a waterside terrace, is delightful. But the amazing thing about Gien is the way it has been so authentically and winsomely restored after wholesale destruction during the Second World War. In fact, if one didn't know that this had happened, it would take a keen eye to discern it.

Approach Gien from the D951 along the south bank, if you can, for a great view of the town and Château. Cross the Loire over the town's 16th-century stone bridge which itself was bombed by the RAF in 1944 as they tried to cut off German supply lines; it has been so well restored that you wouldn't know it. It's best to park somewhere along the waterside on the north bank, and explore the town on foot.

There are fine old red brick houses with herring-bone timbers, along streets ablaze with hanging flower baskets. Climb up to the **Château** which was reconstructed in red brick after massive war damage and is said to be the oldest château in the Loire, having originally been built by Charlemagne in the 8th century. Inside is the **International Hunting and Falconry Museum** which is worth visiting mainly for its exhibitions demonstrating the evolution of hunting from prehistoric times, thus putting in context the modern pastime of *la chasse* which is so fundamental a part of rural life in the area.

Musée International de la Chasse à Tir et de la Fauconnerie, Château de Gien.
Tel: 38 67 69 69
Opening times: daily, Apr-Nov 9.30am-6.30pm, Mar and Dec 10am-noon and 2-5pm;
closed Jan and Feb
Admission: adult 23F; child 15F

To visit the **Faience Museum** and factory, return to the riverside Quai Lenoir, and follow it along to Place Victoire at the western end. A small museum exhibits examples of the handmade deep blue glazed pottery which has been made in the town since 1821, when the factory was founded. Visitors can trace the evolution of the *bleu de Gien* from the early intricate work through to the sought-after modern dinner services. Small single plates and other pieces are for sale at fairly reasonable prices.

Musée de Faïence, Place Victoire. Tel: 38 67 00 05
Opening times: daily 9.30am-noon and 1.45-6pm
If you are interested in visiting the factory itself, this should be arranged in advance by
contacting the museum. Visits are Mondays to Fridays only
Admission: adult 15F; child 10F

MEUNG-SUR-LOIRE

If you are fascinated by the unspeakable cruelty of feudal life, **Meung Château** is one of the less-visited châteaux which you should not miss. Dominating the small, fortified town of Meung-sur-Loire on the north bank of the Loire downstream from

Orléans, this is a rather curious château. It looks austere and forbidding as you arrive at the 13th-century portal, impenetrable walls and sturdy towers surrounded by a dry moat.

The guided tour, with leaflets in English, takes you down underground to the dungeons where prisoners were horrifically tortured and left to starve to death in *oubliette* cells. But there's more to the Château than the mediaeval fortress. It's actually rather a curious mixture, having been the official residence of the Bishops of Orléans (some of whom had their opponents tortured to death) from the 12th century, through the Renaissance, to the French Revolution; much of it was rebuilt in the 18th century. There are many fine and unlikely pieces of furniture, such as a set of English Chippendale chairs. In one room is a collection of weapons spanning the Château's history from crossbows through to Second World War rifles.

Château de Meung, Meung-sur-Loire. Tel: 38 44 36 47
Opening times: daily 9.30am-5pm May 1 to Nov 11, and weekends and public hols the rest of the year
Admission: adult 25F; children free

> For an unusually anarchic sort of lunch, try **Le Rabelais** on Rue du Dr Henri-Michel in Meung-sur-Loire. The coarse, witty, wine-loving 16th-century writer-monk, François Rabelais himself, would have approved of it. There are no frills - you just pay your money and eat as much as you want from a buffet with plenty of salads and cold meats. No need to over-pile your plates, as you can go back for more as often as you like or are able to. It's a great place to take children – especially hungry ones.

Kayaking down the Loire is an entertaining way to spend a couple of hours if you're feeling adventurous. The **Kayak Club de Beaugency** has come up with the bright idea of allowing you to hire a kayak in Meung and float downstream to the pleasant little town of Beaugency where you return it. No previous experience of canoeing is needed and it is a wonderful way to see a lovely stretch of the river as well as being great fun. You are simply carried down by the flow, steering where necessary with a paddle. The distance is roughly 8 kilometres and it takes about half an hour. Obviously, this is very much a fair weather activity, and is best done in swimming gear. One drawback is that you need somebody to drop and collect you, though it may be possible to get a lift in the club's minibus as it returns kayaks upstream.

The Kayak Club de Beaugency does not offer the trips at precise times, but representatives are there on the quayside in Meung and Beaugency for most of the summer.
Tel: 38 44 53 51. One-man kayaks cost 80F, 2- and 3-man kayaks 150F. Suitable for children from about eight upwards.

Kayaking from Meung to Beauregard

☆ ORLEANS

Along with Angers and Tours, Orléans is one of the three large cities of the Loire Valley, and the only one not boasting a château. First impressions are of modern precincts, fashionable shops and cafés overflowing onto wide boulevards. At its heart is the huge and unmistakable Sainte-Croix Cathedral. Marcel Proust described it as 'the ugliest church in France'. Those who see beauty in Chambord would probably disagree.

Orléans has a bloody history. Destroyers of the city include Julius Caesar, Attila the Hun, the English during the Hundred

Years War (less successfully thanks to Joan of Arc), the Prussians and, most disastrously, German bombers in 1940 and the liberating Allies four years later. Surviving examples of ancient Orléans have been left delicately in their places by town planners: a few Gothic church façades and occasional fine old noblemen's townhouses looking like museum pieces. Even the alleys and winding lanes of the picturesque old town on the riverside make up an area too small to get lost in.

Joan of Arc is everywhere. The city's most famous heroine not only has a museum dedicated to her life and heroics, but there's also a Rue Jeanne d'Arc main street, a series of stained glass windows in the cathedral telling her story, a statue of her at prayer outside the *Hôtel de Ville* and another of her on horseback presiding over the magnificent fountains of Place du Martroi, and countless cafés Jeanne d'Arc dotted around town.

Every May 8th there is a *Fête Jeanne d'Arc* to celebrate the Siege of Orléans. Processions through the city are led by a latter-day 'Jeanne' in a full coat of armour astride a white horse, amid flags, banners, fireworks, trumpeting and triumphant cheers. At other times of the year, Orléans is worth visiting for its benign, welcoming atmosphere, and for the collection of excellent museums which stand in for the historical sights which have been destroyed.

Orléans' large **Tourist Office**, which offers information on both the city and surrounding Loiret district, is on Place Albert I, opposite the railway station in the city centre; tel: 38 53 05 95.

Even if you feel put off by the unharmonious riot of wedding-cake towers, jagged pinnacles and hideous gargoyles, it would be a pity to miss a visit to the **Cathédrale Sainte-Croix** as the interior is much more inspiring. Its vast dimensions create a sense of awe, and there is a powerful aura around the Joan of Arc chapel, next to which are plaques remembering the dead of two World Wars. The big, stained glass windows depicting St. Joan's antics are rather more profane.

Also worth looking out for are the beautiful 18th-century woodcarving in the choir, the 13th-century gold and silver chalices in the treasury, and the deep, cool, atmospheric crypt.

The Cathedral is open every day. There are no published opening or closing times but it does close between noon and 2pm. Leaflets are available in English. In the afternoons there are guided tours of the crypt and treasury, for which there is a 10F charge.

River traffic on the Loire near Orléans

The **Maison Jeanne d'Arc** squeezes everything it can out of associations with the heroine. The tall, fine, timber-framed house is a reconstruction on the foundations of the one where the heroine herself stayed in 1429. The original collapsed when the Place du Général de Gaulle, on which it stands, was flattened by German bombers in 1940.

The tour starts with an animated audio-visual show, which puts you concisely into the historical picture. The peasant girl Joan believed that she had a divine mission to save France from English domination, and succeeded in having the Dauphin Charles VII crowned King of France. She was eventually burned at the stake by the English and was canonised in 1920. Her finest hour, however, was the culmination of the 1428-29 Siege of Orléans when by sheer military audacity she forced the English to surrender Orléans, and entered the city in triumph. The event is as important a landmark in French history as the Battle of Hastings is in English.

The 45-minute tour of the house takes you through rooms full of models in armour and other period costume, all kinds of weapons including some extraordinary wind-up contraptions for hurling boulders at the enemy, and documents of the time. The commentary is excellent for those who understand French.

Maison Jeanne d'Arc, Place Général de Gaulle. Tel: 38 42 25 45
Opening times: May-Oct 10am-noon and 2-6pm, Nov-Apr 2-6pm only; closed Mon all year
Admission: adult 9F, children free

The **Musée Historique** is housed in a small characterful Renaissance mansion, stuffed with works of art from across the centuries, inspired by and illustrating the city's history. It starts on the ground floor with an amazing collection of beautifully crafted Gallo-Roman bronze statues of animals and dancing figures discovered and excavated in 1861 from a pagan temple at Neury-en-Sullias 20km away – the terrifying expressions on the faces of the horse and wild boar are masterpieces. Upstairs are some mediaeval ceramics, ivory figures and a few other motley pieces including (inevitably) some scrappy bits of Joan of Arc memorabilia such as a shred of her standard. The top floor is dedicated to local folkloric art and handicrafts, some local goldware and a collections of clocks from over the ages.

Musée Historique, Hôtel Cabu, Place Abbé Desnoyers. Tel: 38 53 39 22
Opening times: 10am-noon and 2-6pm all year; closed Tues
Admission: free Sun morning and Wednes; 9F at all other times; children free

There is not much of an *orléannais* dimension to the **Musée des Beaux Arts**, but the gallery contains one of the finest collections of art in the Loire Valley. A lift takes you up to the second floor of the modern building, from where you can work your way downwards chronologically. Start with some 14th- and 15th-century sculptures and religious paintings, leading into some wonderful Renaissance art; look out for Tintoretto's 'Portrait of a Venetian' and Velázquez's stunning 'St Thomas'. Among the Impressionist art is Gauguin's 'Fête Gloanec'. The Pastel Gallery has a rare collection of portraits and busts including some by Pigalle.

Musée des Beaux Arts, 1, rue Ferdinand Rabier. Tel: 38 53 39 22
Opening times: 10am-noon and 2-6pm all year; closed Tues
Admission: free Sun morning and Wednes; 14F at all other times; children free

PARC FLORAL DE LA SOURCE

The Loiret is an underground river which bubbles out of the flat landscape south of the Loire, just 18 kilometres from of its confluence with the Loire, a little way downstream of Orléans. In the watery world around the river's rather extraordinary source is the 75-acre Parc Floral, home to waterfowl, cranes and a few flamingos which stand nonchalantly about on their matchstick legs.

The park's more famous attraction is the vast expanse of flowerbeds in what is both a giant nursery and a colossal garden with rockeries, fountains, ponds and bushy copses. From the end of March the park erupts in a riot of hundreds of thousands of spring flowers, which a couple of months later give way to azaleas and rhododendrons. Then in summer, there are said to be upwards of half a million roses in bloom before it's time for the September dahlias, followed in the autumn by chrysanthemums of all colours. Gardening lovers have been known to believe themselves in Paradise.

It's a great place for a good walk, too. Follow the vividly green bank of the calm, slow-flowing Loiret, watching the exotic birds

Parc Floral de la Source

and flocks of wild geese which occasionally take to the air en masse, wings abeat, forming a graceful, seemingly single figure. Upstream, towards the great spring itself, the park becomes wilder and less formal; it's well worth continuing towards the extremity of the park, beyond the river, into a wood of huge, ancient trees. You may spot some fallow deer, camouflaged in the undergrowth.

Back in the more regimented areas of the park, don't miss walking down some of the long, straight avenues of gravel, slicing through the endless abundance of colour and floral scent – it's as different an experience from viewing the expanses of blooms from afar as gliding along in a sailing boat is from watching a regatta from the shore. A good place to finish a walking tour of the park is at the beautiful *miroir* half-moon shaped pool.

There's also a horticultural information centre for visitors, and a big, airy, reasonably priced restaurant in a giant conservatory within the park. Children will probably gain most pleasure from the animal park where deer, emus and peacocks wander about and from riding on a little train which runs 20-minute trips round the park. In addition there is mini-golf, a picnic area and a playground.

Parc Floral de la Source, Olivet, Orléans. Tel: 38 63 33 17
Opening times: daily, Apr - mid-Nov 9am-6pm, rest of year 2-5pm only
Admission: adult 16F, child under 12 free

> If you're looking for somewhere to **picnic** near Orléans, there's a delightful spot by an enchanting stone bridge over the Loiret, just outside Olivet. Take the D14 towards St Hilaire–St Mesmin and then either of two turnings down narrow lanes to the right. They converge just before the bridge, where you can park and walk a short way along the grassy bank to find a tranquil spot.

☆ SANCERRE WINE-TASTING

This lovely old hilltop village overlooking the Loire, about a 1½ hour drive up-stream from Orléans, is geographically quite remote from the other suggestions in this chapter, but has been included because it is the home of the Loire Valley's foremost wine. Wine-lovers in the region should not miss the opportunity to climb the steep, picturesque old street looking out for

The Sancerre wine harvest

négociants offering *dégustations*, and perhaps make the most carefully considered wine purchase of the holiday. In the outlying villages, particularly Chavignol and Ménétreuil-sous-Sancerre many more *vignerons* offer free tastings.

Sancerre is a crisp, bone dry, light white wine made from the Sauvignon Blanc grape variety and characterised by the matrix of subtle and delicate tastes which can be discerned within a single mouthful. 'Smokey' and 'spicy' are two adjectives commonly applied to these wines; others are 'gunflinty' and 'catty' – the latter, you might find hard to believe if you haven't yet tasted wines like this, not by any means derogatory.

The light red Sancerres and even lighter rosés are more difficult to find. Neither have anything like the complexity or subtlety of their white counterparts and both tend to be overpriced. The other famous wine grown locally which you will find in Sancerre is Pouilly-Fumé from a distinct wine-growing region with its own *Appellation Controlée*, just across the Loire. The wine is rather like Sancerre in some respects but has a highly individual smokey flavour which wine-makers all over the world try to emulate. Pouilly-Fumé has nothing whatever to do with Burgundy's very expensive Pouilly-Fussé.

The quickest way to Sancerre from Orléans is to follow the D952 along the north bank of the Loire, crossing over onto the D955 at Cosné-Cours-sur-Loire. However, there is a slower, more scenic route on the D951 and D751 meandering through the pretty villages of the south bank. For Chavignol, take the D1183 a couple of kilometres out of Sancerre, and for Ménétreuil-sous-Sancerre, follow the twisting main road down from Sancerre towards the river: the village is at the bottom of the hill.

ST BENOIT ABBEY

The abbey at St Benoît, in the quiet, shady village of St Benoît-sur-Loire upriver from Orléans, is one of the most beautiful and powerfully atmospheric Romanesque churches to be found anywhere. Here are believed to lie the remains of St Benedict, founder of the Benedictine order, which were brought from Italy to a monastery on the same spot a century after his death in 547 AD; it soon became a site of mass pilgrimage. The present abbey church, or 'Basilique' as it is signposted, was built between the 11th and 13th centuries and survived despite the destruction of the monastery buildings after the French Revolution.

One unmissable feature is the stone-carved pillars in the 11th-century porch, depicting biblical scenes made up of characters with wonderfully expressive faces ranging from menacing demonic stares, through impish grins, to the blissful serenity of the blessed. The nave and choir, dating from the following century, have a cavernous, airy feel with high vaulting and light streaming in and reflecting off the white stone walls and pillars.

But the climax of a visit to St Benoît is descending into the crypt where the chest containing St Benedict's relics lies in hushed reverence. The aura reaches its height every day at 6.15pm when the cowled monks in their white habits, who have noiselessly floated in for prayer, gently disperse the silence with their ethereal Gregorian plainchant, to the low, hovering notes of an organ. Perhaps only Solesmes matches the atmosphere of deep spirituality.

Basilique St Benoît, St Benoît-sur-Loire. Tel: 38 35 72 43
Open all the time, all year round
Vespers are sung every evening in Gregorian plainchant at 6.15, lasting about 25 minutes. Visitors are welcome to participate, provided of course that they arrive before the start and remain respectful. Mass is sung in the church at 10.45am on Sunday and feast days and at 11.45am on other days
No admission charge

The tiny 9th-century church of **Germigny-des-Près**, 5 kilometres from St Benoît, is a highly recommended stop for anybody heading upriver from Orléans. It is believed to be one of the oldest churches in France and is adorned with brilliant mosaics; however, it is the deeply peaceful atmosphere for which you will remember it most.

☆ SOLOGNE DRIVE

The Sologne is something of an anomaly in the Loire Valley. Even though it is bordered by the great river, the historic cities of Blois and Orléans to the north, and the Cher tributary to the south, the region seems to hide away from the grand, affluent valley with its fabulous castles and fertile plains. The Sologne was avoided, except as a hunting forest, by the royalty and warriors of the Middle Ages and then by the great builders of the Renaissance age. Consequently, once you get away from the great hunting châteaux such as Chambord and Cheverny on the edge of the forest, as described in Day Six, the Sologne is largely free of sights. The Loire Valley's hundreds of thousands of annual visitors tend to perpetuate the tradition of ignoring it. The fact that walking in the region is made very difficult doesn't help; there are numerous inviting-looking tracks leading off into the forest, but these usually lead to the impenetrable hedges and barbed wire of private property with unwelcoming *Passage Interdit* signs.

As the *Musée Solognot* in Romorantin (see Day Six) explains so evocatively, the sparse population of the region has always led a very different sort of life from its neighbours in the fecund parts of the Loire Valley. For generations *Solognots* squeezed an impoverished living out of land which had constantly to be reclaimed by dredging and drainage. They have a reputation for being inward-looking and superstitious; traditionally, outsiders regarded them with unease amid rumours of witchcraft and strange rituals.

A tour of the Sologne through villages dotted around the forests, lakes and wet heathland provides a striking contrast for anybody on the Loire château trail.

Leaving Orléans via the southern suburb of Olivet, take the minor D15 towards the village of Jouy-le-Potier, a typical hub

Life in the Sologne remains mainly rural

village of the Sologne, where the land is slightly raised and dyke-top roads converge like spokes into clusters of sturdy, squat, tim-ber-framed red-brick houses above which rise rustic steepled churches.

Turn left onto the D18 for la Ferté-St Aubin where there is a beautiful moated château surrounded by a park. Then head back west on the D61 across the flat landscape of forest broken up by orchards and asparagus beds towards Ligny-le-Ribault and Yvoy-le-Marron. These villages are delightful places to stop for a drink in the village square and watch the small-scale agricultural way of life going on around you. You may see some *paysannes* in wide-brimmed straw hats on their way out to water their aspara-gus or men shuffling into town for a glass of wine at the café, still wearing their traditional *sabots* (clogs, suitable for slipping on and off in marshy terrain).

Straight ahead on the D35 is larger Chaumont-sur-Tharonne with a lovely 15th-century church and the excellent La Croix Blanche hotel and restaurant (see 'Where to Stay'). From here take the very narrow D123 which takes you slowly down to St Viâtre and the watery world of hundreds of *étangs*. These myriad

Château de la Ferté-St Aubin in the Sologne

lakes are all different – some of them open, marshy and stagnant, others secluded in the forest and carpeted with waterlilies.

From St Viâtre take the D49 through some of the marshiest parts of the Sologne, down to Marcilly-en-Gault, then on along the D122 to Millancay. From here you can go right and follow the main D922 back towards Orléans or turn left for Romorantin.

WHERE TO STAY

Beaugency
🏠 ✕ 🛏 *££*

Hôtel de l'Abbaye, *F-45190*
Beaugency
Tel: 38 44 67 35
Open all year
A rare opportunity to stay in an historic monument. The spacious grey stone public areas of this 17th-century abbey turned into an hotel have a characterful but rather spartan atmosphere. Some of the bedrooms are very spacious with high ceilings; others are pokey little former cells, though all are well equipped. The dining room is long and narrow with every table overlooking the Loire; in sum-

mer you can eat outside on a terrace. Food is wholesome and traditional, with a good selection of gamey dishes from the Sologne. Last orders: lunch 2pm; dinner 10pm.

Chaumont-sur-Tharonne
🏠 ✕ 🛏 *£££*

La Croix Blanche, *5, place Mottu, F-41600 Chaumont-sur-Tharonne*
Tel: 54 88 55 12
Open all year
At the hub of five roads converging from across the Sologne, this is a hotel with a restaurant which specialises in being *Solognot* to the core. The stuffed heads of stags and boar

look down from the restaurant walls as you choose from a menu of countless different kinds of game - hare pâté, *civet* of quail, roast boar, wild goose, and so on. And yet, somewhat incongruously, there's nothing remotely rustic about the elegant bedrooms or the slick service. If you stop here for just a cup of coffee, it will be served on a lace doily with a bowl of chocolates. Last orders: lunch 1.30pm; dinner 9.30pm.

Gien
🏠 ✕ 🛏 *££*

Hôtel du Rivage, *1 quai de Nice, F-45500 Gien*
Tel: 38 67 20 53
Closed mid-Feb - mid-Mar
A chic, very tastefully decorated little hotel down by the waterfront with lovely views over the river and old hump-backed stone bridge. The bedrooms are spacious and comfortable; the ones overlooking the river in particular are excellent value for money. The cooking is modern with a *nouvelle cuisine*-ish attention to detail, but served in generous portions. You are expected to eat there if you are staying in the hotel, although there seems to be no hard and fast rule about this. Last orders: lunch 2pm; dinner 9.15pm.

Nouan-le-Fuzelier
🏠 ✕ 🛏 *££*

Le Moulin de Villiers, *Nouan-le-Fuzelier, F-41600 Lamotte-Beuvron*
Tel: 54 88 72 27
Closed Jan-end Mar, first 2 wks Sept; Tues eve & Wednes Nov-Dec
A converted watermill on a Sologne lake surrounded by forest. There is a real feeling of peace, despite being only a short distance from the main

north-south N20. The bedrooms are simple, but pleasant, as is the restaurant which is popular with locals and specialises in game. There is a lakeside terrace where you can have an *apéritif* in summer. Last orders: lunch 2pm; dinner 8.45pm.

Olivet
🏠 ✕ 🛏 *£££*

Les Quatre Saisons, *351, rue de la Reine Blanche, F-45160 Olivet*
Tel: 38 66 14 30
R closed Sun eve and Tues Oct-Mar
This really is somewhere rather special as a place both to stay and to eat. In summer meals are served on a verandah overlooking an enchanted

stretch of the Loiret; for less clement weather, the main dining room is a large and very bright former dance-hall. The speciality is fish and seafood as evidenced by the large salt-water tank where lobsters and crayfish swim around awaiting their fate. Rooms are all individually and very tastefully decorated and equipped, many of them with delightful views over the wooded banks of the river. Last orders: lunch 2pm; dinner 9.30pm.

WHERE TO EAT

Briaré

✗ ▬ ££

Hostellerie Canal, 19, rue de Pont-Canal, Briaré
Tel: 38 31 22 54
Closed Dec 15-Jan 15 and Mon Oct - mid-June
Briaré is a pleasant little town a short way upstream from Gien, where an aqueduct takes a canal over the Loire. Guests at the Hostellerie Canal have a fine view of this, both from the terrace where you can eat in summer and from the attractive main dining room. The menu is fish-based and traditional, and there is an extensive cheeseboard with some extremely strong *chèvres*. Last orders: lunch 2pm; dinner 9pm.

La Ferté-St Aubin

✗ ▬ £

Ferme la Lande, Route de Marcilly, la Ferté-St Aubin
Tel: 38 76 64 37
Closed Sun eve, Mon and second 2 wks Aug
An atmospheric old *Solognot* house on the D921 a couple of kilometres outside La Ferté St Aubin. Asparagus, game and other typical Sologne food is served in an unpretentious, no frills way and offers good value for money. There is a reasonably priced list of mainly Loire wines, including some excellent reds to complement the gamey dishes. Last orders: lunch 1.30pm; dinner 8.30pm.

Orléans

✗ ▬ ££££

La Crémaillère, 34, rue de Notre Dame de Recouvrance, Orléans
Tel: 38 53 49 17
Closed Sun eve, Mon and Aug
Locals claim that this is not only the city's foremost restaurant but also one of the best in the entire Loire Valley. The award of two Michelin rosettes lends some credence to this view. Gourmets wax lyrical about the fresh, delicate sauces which bring out the very best in the fish and seafood dishes, and about the mouthwatering selection of puddings. The presentation is elegant but not over-elaborate, letting the food speak for itself. Similarly, this superlative restaurant's decor and ambience is one of relative simplicity. Last orders: lunch 2pm; dinner 9.30pm.

St Thibault

✗ £

L'Etoile, 2, quai de Loire, St Thibault, Sancerre
Tel: 48 54 12 15
Closed Dec-Feb; Wednes except Jul and Aug
This is the place to eat if you are in Sancerre for the day. St Thibault is just 4km out of town, on the west bank of the river. L'Etoile is a small restaurant (so be sure to book) in a wonderful setting with all tables enjoying river views. In summer you can eat out on the terrace. The food is regional and traditional with gamey terrines and pâtés, and plenty of Loire fish. There is also a small hotel across the road under the same management, but this isn't recommended. Last orders: lunch 2pm; dinner 9pm.